For Katelyn Jenné, my favorite teenage daughter,

for Robert, my reason for having our favorite teenage daughter,

and for mothers everywhere, who never stop loving.

Contents

Chapter 5
Her Emerging Sexuality 101

Shame or Celebration ★ Go Ask Your Sister ★ Prepare Yourself ★ Sexual Health Isn't Just Physical ★ Teaching Abstinence ★ The Big "M" Word ★ Risky Sex ★ Sex Sells ★ Promoting Healthy Sexuality ★ Warning Signs ★ Stretching Exercises ★ Exercise: Sex 101 ★ Exercise: Take a Research Trip ★ Exercise: Raise a Critical Thinker ★ Exercise: Write a "Sexual Code of Conduct"

Chapter 6
Promoting a Healthy Lifestyle 127

A Balance of Activities ★ Letting Go of Her Responsibility ★ Monster in the Mirror ★ Everyone Else Was Doing It: Drugs, Alcohol, and Peer Pressure ★ A Healthy Heart and Soul ★ Warning Signs ★ Stretching Exercises ★ Exercise: Balancing the Wheel of Life ★ Exercise: What I Wouldn't Change List ★ Exercise: Personal Choice Inventory ★ Exercise: Pressure Response

Chapter 7
Forming Positive Relationships 149

Her Relationship Choices ★ Through Thick and Thin ★ Rejection: Not Feeling Good Enough ★ Confident and Assertive ★ Thinking about Romantic Relationships ★ Warning Signs ★ Stretching Exercises ★ Exercise: Awareness Lists ★ Exercise: My First-Aid Kit for a Broken Heart ★ Exercise: Self-Defense and Assertiveness-Training Classes ★ Exercise: Keep on Nurturing

Chapter 8
Succeeding in School 173

Making the Adjustment ★ School Moms ★ Making the Grade ★ School Responsibility: Learning the Hard Way ★ Skipping: The Great Escape ★ Putting Her School and Teachers to the Test ★ Exercise: How Well Does Your Daughter's School Measure Up? ★ When to Advocate, When to Step Back ★ Warning Signs ★ Stretching Exercises ★ Exercise: Pony Express Rewards ★ Exercise: Plan a "Play Day"

Chapter 9
Discovering an Identity 187

Finding Her Own Way ★ The Four Identity Decisions ★ By Word and Deed ★ Warning Signs ★ Stretching Exercises ★ Exercise: Guess Who's Coming to Dinner ★ Exercise: And Once I Dreamed ★ Exercise: Change the World

Chapter 10
A Final Message 197

What Your Daughter Wants You to Know but May Never Tell You ★ No Greater Happiness than This ★ Stretching Exercises ★ Exercise: Good Night Affirmations

References 201

Resources 205

Crisis Support ★ Prevention ★ Addiction ★ Eating Disorders ★ Health ★ Family Education ★ Alternative Teen Magazines

Acknowledgments

First, I would like to thank all the mothers and daughters who so kindly contributed their experience, wisdom, and humor to this book. Even though you are too numerous to name, you were an inspiration to me and I appreciate each and every one of you.

I want to thank all the strong, smart young women whom I've had the privilege to counsel over the last several years. I appreciate your consistent willingness to "tell it like it is" and for sharing your insights, heartaches, and creativity. Your extremely entertaining personalities made my work a joy. I treasure the hours we spent together.

To Angela Watrous, my first editor at New Harbinger, whose persistence and enthusiasm helped launch this book. Thank you for all the time you spent collaborating with me in the initial stages of this project. I am grateful to the New Harbinger staff, especially Amy Shoup, Heather Garnos, and Brady Kahn for their creative contributions. It was a pleasure working with you and knowing my book was in such good hands.

I would like to thank those friends who were especially helpful to me while writing this book. First to Kathryn Wilson and Maureen Thrash for sharing their expertise as mothers and encouragement as friends. I want to thank Rhoda Weber for being a valued godmother to my daughter and a wise and loving fairy godmother to me, and

Susan Jorgensen, who has blessed me with her enthusiasm, support, and humor since my career as a writer and mother began. I am a happier person and healthier mom for knowing all of you.

I am especially grateful to my cousin, Corinne Marie. Thank you for supporting this writing project the way you support everything I do.

Motherhood is made so much easier with a loving extended family. I want to thank my sister Sherie and my parents and in-laws for all you do.

And finally, I must thank my husband and daughter, the two people I love the most in the world. I am especially grateful to my husband for the system he developed to help organize my piles of writing and consequently complete this book with less stress, and to my daughter, who was a constant inspiration for new ideas (whether she knows it or not).

Preface

Four years ago I was sitting in a bathroom stall at Disneyland when I realized I had been there before. In fact I realized it was the same spot where I had perched thirty years earlier. It was the very spot where I had started my period for the first time. Some 339 menstrual cycles later, I had returned quite by accident. It was a thirty-year reunion of sorts for my reproductive system.

Most women remember where they were the first time they started their period. And I'm sure if we took a poll we'd find hundreds of girls who discovered their periods for the first time at Disneyland. But everyone's experience is unique, and what I recall most is the way my mother reacted to the news. It was her reaction that I reflected on in the stall that day, and, as I sat there, I made a silent vow to behave differently when my own daughter broke the news to me.

I remember I was thirteen. We had been in the magical kingdom for several hours before I admitted to the group of relatives we were with that I didn't feel well. They assumed it was the blistering heat and spinning teacups that hadn't agreed with me. I didn't quite know what was going to happen once I got to the rest room, only that it seemed like the right place to go.

It was hot and humid, and the smell was stifling inside the ladies' room. I remember trying to hold my breath to avoid the heavy blanket of odors, soured from the heat. The fact that I couldn't only added to my distress. I had just taken my seat in the stall when I saw it. My head swirled and my heart raced. The loud chorus of flushing toilets made it hard to think straight. Was that what I thought it was?

I heard the familiar laugh of my mother and aunt in between the sound of paper towels being cranked down like slot machines in Las Vegas. I called to my mother through the crack in my door. As discreetly as possible, in a whisper really, I told her that I needed a pad. She looked at me through the crack, her eyes squinted. She said she couldn't hear a thing I was saying and asked me to speak up. In slow motion I silently mouthed each word, so the occupants in the stalls next to me wouldn't hear.

"Deb!" she screamed. "You *couldn't* have!"

For a split second, I believed her. So I checked my underwear again. But there was no denying it. Why was she denying it? My mother had managed to alert the masses to the crisis in my stall.

Flushing ceased. Faucets shut off. Babies stopped crying and chattering women were brought to a standstill. There was nothing but silence and my mom screaming out to my aunt, "Deb started her period! She needs a *pad*, can you believe it?"

Mine was a global announcement. Tourists from all over the world sat right alongside me. China, Africa, and all of Wisconsin would know by sunset. The color of my face now matched my blood-stained underwear. I leaned to the right as far as I could, trying to dodge the crack in the door where I was certain hundreds of eyes were now peering.

I sat in the stall for as long as I could bear it and recited a revised Girl Scout oath. "On my honor, I will do my best, to never announce to Disneyland that my daughter started her period." I will not do that, I pledged to myself as I sat blushing in the stall. I asked myself, "How many females are there in the world? How many eventually start their periods? What's the big deal?" When I left I peeled the tissue seat cover off the back of my numb and sweaty thighs, and emerged to a new crowd of people who thankfully hadn't heard the news yet.

But then I was quickly herded back into the bowels of the bathroom by a pack of my female cousins. They fired questions at me like a barrage of bullets. "Is it true? Did you *start*? Did you get blood on your shorts? Why didn't you want to come out?" and from the youngest, "Look at the mark the toilet ring left on the back of her legs!" I responded only once and said, "No big deal. Forget it." I impressed myself with how cool and sophisticated I sounded.

The truth is I didn't forget it for a minute. Part of me was also secretly ecstatic to be officially a "woman," and when I thought about it, a surge of excitement welled up deep inside me. It was a new beginning and I was thrilled to be growing up.

When my daughter calmly broke the news to me that she had started her period, I practically burst into tears from the shock. "I can't believe it!" I exclaimed. "I just can't believe it!" In my enthusiasm I started planning a "Cinco de Mayo" party in her honor. My flustered husband asked if he should run out and buy flowers, while I searched wildly for pads.

"Mom." My daughter whispered firmly, gripping my upper arm. "Relax." I tried to tell her how exciting this rite of passage was, about the glory of womanhood, the joy of fertility. But her grip only tightened. This time, in slow motion, it was my daughter who silently mouthed her words in exaggerated fashion: *"It's - no - big - deal."* And I saw on her face that expression I had also once worn, an expression that said, "It's no big deal. Don't make it into one."

A wave of composure suddenly poured over me. "Yes, you're right," I lied.

It hit me. I had broken the vow I had made at my reunion in the bathroom stall at Disneyland. I'd meant to behave differently with my daughter.

It was then that I forgave my mom for her unbridled exuberance in the Disneyland bathroom. Now that I'm on the other side of the mother/daughter relationship, I've lightened up.

I have continued to watch my daughter go through more changes. With every change, I have had to learn how to adjust to a new daughter. I needed to be ready for her to regress when she needed to, and soar when she was able. I needed to understand her world as different from mine. I needed to learn how to guide her, not as a child but as a young woman starting on her journey to independence. Finally, I needed to learn how not to embarrass her.

How you help your adolescent daughter move through these years and reach her full potential *is* a big deal. The quality of your relationship is a big deal. But when she says it's not, don't argue. By the time she reaches your age, she'll probably agree with you. You can never know where she'll be when she finally realizes you were right.

Introduction

When I told my thirteen-year-old daughter that the topic of my next book was going to be a guide for moms who wanted to help their adolescent daughters build healthy lives, she looked long and hard at me with a deeply troubled expression on her face. It took me a minute to discern the negative reaction from the thrilled and jubilant one I had expected.

And then she said, "Uh, Mom? You need to *read* a book about that, not *write* it."

After I recovered from the shock, I shot back in my own defense, "I do have special training in this, you know." When I saw she wasn't the least bit impressed, I added, "But I'm not writing this as an expert! I'm writing it as a mom who still needs to figure out a lot, too." I was telling the truth, even though I hadn't admitted it to myself yet.

"Good," she said with a dramatic sigh of relief. "I can relax now."

For the next twenty minutes I obsessed internally about how our perceptions of the relationship we shared and the mother I was could be so different. After so many years as a counselor to teens and their families, I thought I had some expertise that even she would readily acknowledge, but the truth is, when it comes to raising your own daughter, no one is an expert. In our daughters' adolescent years most of us discover that.

I did not set out to conduct clinical research with this project. Instead, my goal was to hear what was in the hearts and minds of mothers and daughters and to learn from their life experiences. Over a period of two years, I formed discussion groups with adolescent girls from a variety of ethnic and socioeconomic backgrounds and family structures. I also met with girls individually and sent out questionnaires across the country and abroad.

My process of data collection was far from scientific, but those who shared their deepest thoughts and feelings with me were rich in wisdom, inspiration, and humor. I laughed a lot while writing this book. Adolescent girls are incredibly witty and fun. I quickly learned that comic relief is absolutely essential to this topic. Mothers and daughters demonstrated what powerful effects laughter could have in their lives. They shared how important it was to spend time having fun together. There were heartaches to be shared, too. Experiencing some pain during this period seems to be unavoidable, but as I learned, difficult times can result in important new insights for mothers and daughters alike.

BRIDGE OF NO RETURN

At every stage, being a mother is hard work. And, at every stage, so is being a child. Somewhere between the ages of ten and twenty, girls cross a bridge. It's a bridge that most mothers say seems to be constructed of wooden planks loosely connected in midair, swinging wildly with every step their daughters must take across a jungle of unknown dangers and raging rivers.

Some adolescent daughters show a fair amount of balance crossing the bridge. Others find ingenious ways to hang on and steady themselves. A few will fall and be rescued from the rushing rapids, and even fewer will not make it at all. Some will freeze and find themselves immobilized in the middle. But one way or another, all girls set out to venture across the bridge in their own style and at their own pace.

Mothers watch, worry, hope, and pray that the bridge will be strong enough to bring them to safety and security. Some mothers try to prevent their daughters from taking the journey; others pack their bags and seem to want to make the trip for them. Yet others wonder sadly why their daughters have to cross the bridge at all.

But the truth is, for all girls, the bridge is theirs to cross, not ours. And even though some are small, and some bridges are shaky, they will cross their bridge just as we did.

A mother described the memory of her own crossing:

> It was a long, slow, shaky, and uncertain bridge. I crossed it alone for the most part. In fact, no one seemed to notice I was even on it until my thirteenth birthday, when all my family's gifts were personal items centered around my developing "bust" and soon to be menstruating body. I was not amused. I would have preferred the white frosted lipstick, hot pink and orange diary, and Jimi Hendrix albums I had eagerly requested. I guess my family understood I was about to embark on a new stage of development, and they were preparing me in the only way they knew how. But it made no sense to me at the time. I only felt more alone and embarrassed about the changes I was facing. I didn't want to cross that bridge. I wanted to hide and pretend I wasn't even on it.

Most mothers want to find better ways to help their daughters grow up. They want to spare them the kind of awkwardness and embarrassment they may have experienced as teens. And while mothers can't change the shape of the journey, they can equip their daughters with a new and revolutionary resource: *themselves*.

LABOR PAINS THE SECOND TIME AROUND

From her journal, the mother of a fifteen-year-old daughter wrote:

> There are days when it feels like a thousand miles stretch between my daughter and me. At times, when she moves a part of herself further away from me, I find myself clamoring to cross this great divide between us. I can't always find a way to reach her the way I use to when she was younger. I doubt myself as a mother and then wonder how well I really even know her. Up until now, being a mother has been so easy for me. What happened?

Like everything in life, your relationship with your daughter is in a constant state of change. Regardless of how wonderful your relationship may be, there comes a time in every mother's life when you wonder how well you really know your daughter.

You wonder because the boundaries of your relationship suddenly seem so different. You don't understand as much about your daughter for the simple reason that she doesn't tell you as much. And there may be walls protecting thoughts and feelings where there once were none. Your daughter's moods can fluctuate in as much time as it takes you to walk across the living-room floor. The talkative, enthusiastic young girl who just moments earlier happily greeted you after school can miraculously transform herself into your worst nightmare.

Raising an adolescent may feel like giving birth all over again. It's true that being a mother who cares is sometimes painful. Being a mother who cares too much can be torture. But being a mother who works hard at what she does is a guaranteed job for life. It is a position with both great job security and *insecurity*. The benefits are inconsistent and they fluctuate like the stock market. There is some training for this career for those women who have been fortunate enough to learn from their own mothers what to do and what not to do. Others learn from friends, siblings, and, hopefully, books like this one.

But such training can only do so much. Day-to-day experience is usually a better teacher. I haven't met a mother yet who didn't incorporate her intuitive and creative abilities to make her job easier and more fun. But most mothers still find they muddle through, a day at a time, with their children. Love, it would seem, is the greatest teacher of all.

Still, love is not always enough. Just as you think you've established a comfortable way of life with your children, they may very well grow restless and unwilling to accommodate the comfort zone you've found. You find yourself in a job crisis as the role you played so well up to this point now becomes less and less stable.

THE HEARTACHE AND HEARTBURN OF ADOLESCENT DEVELOPMENT

Adolescence is a complicated time of life for many reasons. It's both an exciting and potentially confusing transition to make. No other developmental stage is characterized by such compelling physical, social, and intellectual changes.

Your daughter is striving for adulthood. She is relating to you, or wanting to relate to you, with new independence. She is also relating to her friends with new intimacy, to society with new commitment, and to herself with new understanding. All girls must adjust to their changing body sizes and shapes, to awakening feelings of mature sexuality, and to new ways of thinking. You may notice that your daughter's ideas are more logical and abstract, but that she is also limited by a natural inclination for extreme self-interest. As one mother described it, "They're full of themselves."

During these years young girls must choose from a vast number of sexual, moral, political, religious, and educational paths as they develop their own identities. Girls are extremely receptive to the models they see at home, in school, and in the mass media. Their observations and experiences influence their moral decision-making and behaviors.

Your values and ideals may be a strong influence on your daughter, but her peer group will in all likelihood dominate her music, dress, socializing, and dating preferences. Friends offer a powerful support during this time. Friends may also help girls achieve a higher status, which can encourage positive as well as negative behaviors. For many girls in the adolescent years who "you know" becomes who you are.

There are as many ways to raise daughters as there are daughters to raise, but adolescent girls have a number of characteristics in common. They often stop communicating, lose confidence, and worry about their appearance, friends, boys, and school. Braces, retainers, pimples, bras, and menstrual pads replace new dolls, skates, and teddy bears. Their bodies are changing, sometimes so fast that they can't keep up on the inside with what's happening on the outside. Growing pains ache, physically as well as emotionally. There is loss and there is anticipation for the new. There is excitement mixed with fear. The transition happens whether you, as a mom, are ready or not. In a moment you realize your daughter is someone different. Life changes for everyone.

The turmoil that is experienced between you and your daughter during this time ranges from mild to extreme, but almost everyone agrees it can fluctuate unpredictably. There are times when every mother feels alienated, rudely brushed aside, and genuinely perplexed. When it happens, you may ask yourself, "Why is she screaming at the top of her lungs? What made her suddenly withdraw and ignore me? Why is it that everything I do and say, in her opinion, is wrong? Why is she so critical of the clothes I'm wearing today? Do I look like I need reminding of my aging skin? How did I, her unconditional reservoir of love and support, turn into her very worst enemy?" And finally, "What did I do to deserve this?"

The good news is that you probably did nothing to deserve it, but the bad news is that you might have done something to set it off. The good news is that there's a lot you can do to respond helpfully to the situation. The bad news is that your daughter is not likely to give you any direct clues how to begin.

It's often the case that mothers experience the turbulence of these years more than their daughters do. Girls are less worried than their moms are about most things. For daughters, anxiety and worry are mixed with new love, romance, and dreams for the future. For mothers, anxiety and worry are usually mixed with more anxiety and worry. Daughters buy breath mints; mothers stock up on antacids.

FINDING SOLUTIONS

Though there are a lot of similarities between girls at this age, the timing of these changes varies and is greatly influenced by differences in social and cultural backgrounds. The basic developmental tasks, however, seem to be much the same around the world. One thing is certain: Every daughter can benefit from the understanding a mother often has of the unique and sometimes peculiar ways she relates to the world and to you. No two daughters are alike. "My teenage daughters are as different as night and day", said one mother of three adolescents. "Their responses to life are different, and my relationship with each one is different. What works with one doesn't work with the other. I try to respect the differences by treating them in ways that work best for each of their personalities. So far, it's worked."

There are no "cookie molds" for daughters. That makes your job as a mother all the more exciting and challenging, even though the process is not an easy one. Adjusting to all the changes can be difficult and stressful. There are risks as well as opportunities.

As a mother, you're on your own. And as a mother, you're never alone. Mothers are clearly in plentiful supply, and they share a strong bond. Women need each other in times like this. And yet how many of us would benefit from our collective wisdom if only we had more time?

The purpose of this book is to give you access to some of that wisdom. It is designed to help you connect with others going through similar challenges and to give you specific ideas and approaches to not only help you survive these times but actually help your daughter thrive during these years, growing safe and strong.

Although there are no simple answers or formulas for every challenge you are likely to face, you can develop a positive mind-set about your daughter's development and growth. There are principles you can learn and apply that will help you make your daughter's journey to independence easier.

This book can help you guide your daughter confidently through the process of growing up. Before you can empower your daughter's growth, however, you must empower yourself. As one mother told me: "To know your daughter, know yourself." Therefore, the first part of this book will help you empower yourself to be the best mom you can be, utilizing your own strengths and confidence to inspire hers.

The second half of this book will guide you step-by-step through strategies you can employ to help your daughter navigate through the specific challenges she faces. Each chapter is designed to offer you clear examples of what you can say and do to help her achieve a sense of pride, value, belonging, and purpose in the person she is becoming.

LIFELONG LESSONS

The mother of an eleven-year-old girl told me: "I haven't read a book yet that helps me to know how to instill a sense of resiliency and hope in my daughter—the belief that she can and will get through anything she needs to in life. I often wonder how as mothers we can give them that."

Adolescence is a special time when girls begin to make important life choices for themselves. Mothers still have much to impart, but you have to know how to adjust to your daughter's different thoughts and feelings to have an impact, and you have to be ready for change. It is also important to remember that for most teen girls the adolescent years are happy ones. Every teenage daughter is bound to have some difficulties, but most behaviors that can potentially lead to lifelong or life-threatening harm can be redirected with your support and attention.

As my daughter so readily points out to me, I am not the expert, if one even exists. I was in need of learning too, from her, from other girls her age, from other mothers with adolescent daughters, and from mothers who have been there and back. Readers will have the opportunity to learn from a variety of these "experts." Together, we will show you how to help your daughter discover where her hope and resiliency lies. This confidence will assist your daughter throughout her life.

It is my belief that no developmental path is set in stone. It is also my belief that adolescent daughters can benefit from their mother's positive influence and support, the encouragement of peers, and a spiritual focus that can be an internal compass for life.

Daughters will cross the bridge from girlhood to womanhood with or without you. And once they begin, they rarely look back. Help prepare your daughter for the crossing, and be ready for the roadblocks, detours, dead ends, and breakdowns that may affect her journey. Use this book as a resource. It was written with the hope that you will use the tools between these pages to help your daughter grow happy, healthy, and wise. Most of all, it is my goal that this book will help you experience greater joy as you watch from the banks of the river.

PART

I

Empowering Yourself

**CHAPTER
1**

Accepting Your Daughter's Desire for Independence

*What worries me the most is that we are so close right now.
I just hope middle school and hormones don't mess our relationship up. I don't know how I'll be able to handle it if she grows
away from me. Wanting to buy bras and makeup, meeting boys,
wanting to go to parties, and driving someday! I get a knot in
the pit of my stomach thinking about it. I know she has to grow
up, but a part of me wants to keep her this age forever.*

—Mother of a twelve-year-old daughter

Every step your daughter takes to cross the bridge to adulthood
requires some adjustment on your part. The steps she takes as an
adolescent are as essential to her growth and development as the
first steps she took as a toddler. Your encouragement continues to be
vital to her sense of achievement and success. As your daughter
seeks independence, you must learn to adjust to her changing needs.

Accepting your daughter's desire for independence is often complicated by competing desires you feel for your daughter's physical and emotional well-being, and happiness and your desire to maintain some influence over her life choices and decisions. Some mothers are not ready for the kind of adventures their daughters are seeking as they mature. Others may struggle to adjust to the increased time their daughters want to spend away from them. Or, if you are like many mothers, you may have spent an inordinate amount of time trying to deny what's happening because you love her and it's sad to have your little girl grow up.

MOTHER LOVE, MOTHER LOSS

Motherhood is marked by a series of beginnings and endings. It starts with the creation of one of the most powerful and enduring bonds you can experience in life and changes as your young daughter grows up. The transitions in your daughter's life are varied and numerous, and you must adapt with her.

As a mother you are challenged to let go of the daughter you had and make way for the daughter to come. Just when you have settled into one stage, along comes another. Just when you have connected on one level, your girl rises to a new one. Now your "baby" can *have* a baby. Change is constant even when it moves slowly. You are faced with the realization that nothing is constant or lasts forever.

Mothers I interviewed had a great deal to say about the sense of loss they feel during this stage of life. Some felt estranged from their daughters for the first time. The very act of a teenager's increasing desire for independence and separation might have created tension in the mother/daughter relationship that had not been evident before. Others have told me they routinely experience pangs of grief as they struggle to understand where their "little girl" has gone; some said they have experienced deep conflicts about "letting go" of their daughters. Here are a few of their comments.

Straight Talk from Moms

★ *What happened? When my daughter was a little girl she wanted to be with me every minute of the day! She used to think I was the smartest person alive. Now, she doesn't think I know anything! I'm hopelessly "unhip," old, and out of date! I think back to the little cherub she used to be, showering me with affection, and wonder why it has to come to this. I miss the way it used to be. I know she has to separate from me, but it's just so sad.*

★ *My daughter wants to spend more time with her friends, and I feel excluded. I know that's silly, but it's really hard because I miss her.*

★ *I think of physical changes when I think of how my daughter is emotionally moving away from me. There's just not the physical closeness that we used to share. Like she has no desire for it.*

★ *It's very different now. She used to be all "lovey dovey" and a real "mommy's girl." It used to be that she just wanted me around the most, but now she wants to be with her father. I see that as a positive thing, but it is painful.*

Girls who are growing more independent generally spend more time away from their mothers. Initially, at least, this feels odd. You begin to lose touch with the day-to-day experiences you are used to being so intimately involved with. This distance between you and your daughter may cause you to experience a variety of feelings. It may be difficult to move from being the center of your daughter's world to now finding yourself taking a backseat.

It's difficult to step back from a relationship when you love someone. Even when the parting is not physical, emotional separation can be heartrending. Inevitably the bond most mothers have with their daughter begins to loosen as her world expands. However, not all mothers experience this change as a loss. Many have described what they like and appreciate about their daughter's emerging independence.

Straight Talk from Moms

★ *Since becoming a teenager, my daughter has learned to conquer parts of her temperament that were problematic when she was younger. Consequently, she just keeps becoming more and more enjoyable at this age.*

★ *My daughter lets me into her world more and more now. She's very artistic and musically inclined. She broadens my life with her creativity.*

★ *Adolescence is better for us. My daughter's independence has been a plus for us because she takes more responsibility for herself and I can relax and enjoy our relationship more.*

★ *Everything I love about my daughter just grows more beautiful with time. It's exciting to watch her evolve. I look forward to seeing the life she'll create for herself. There's so much ahead yet!*

Other women have said they were exhausted from years of responsibilities that motherhood demanded. They said seeing their girls reach adolescence was a relief! They were ready for their daughters to take on more independence and responsibility because it gave them a much-needed break.

As is often the case, there are usually opportunities inherent in any life change. However, they are not always easy to find or immediately obvious. You may have already discovered advantages to your daughter's increasing independence or experienced it as sad or frustrating. At the very least, as your daughter maintains less contact with you and has a busier social life, you will need to adjust to a change in your past routines and lifestyle together.

One more possibility exists: the opportunity to grow closer to your daughter instead of further apart. You have the potential to start building a new and different relationship with your daughter from an ending that you may have initially experienced as a loss.

LETTING GO OR GROWING CLOSER

Girls have to grow up and moms have to let go, or do they? Can you give your daughter the freedom to be independent while staying emotionally connected to you in a healthy way? Can you help her separate without actually separating? Adolescence does not have to be about losing. Instead, it can be about embracing change. Learning to renegotiate a changing relationship is not the same as losing it.

Researcher Terri Apter (1990) challenges the notion that during adolescence a girl is trying to separate from her parents. She points out how psychoanalytic theories have influenced how we see our psychological and emotional aims. According to these theories, adult identity is achieved only through separation and individuation. Apter found that adolescents are not so much trying to separate from parents as they are trying to negotiate a new relationship that will work in their new maturity. She believes that the enduring connection between mother and daughter remains a strength, not a sign of immaturity, and when she looked at female adolescent development, she discovered that girls continued to grow from the relationships they had with their parents, just as they continued to care deeply about their parents. Apter contends that teens are trying to influence their mothers' perceptions and worldviews and would much rather maintain a relationship with them than separate from it.

Psychologist Mary Pipher (1994) writes that most girls grow apart from their mothers in junior high and high school. She notes that even at their most vulnerable time, girls reject the help of their mothers, the very individuals who want most to understand their needs. While it's true that you may experience more distance from your daughter than you did before, how you respond to this change may help you grow closer. Oddly, the more you safely let go, the easier it may be for your daughter to remain close to you.

If you are like most moms, you may feel that you don't always handle the transition of separating as smoothly or as graciously as you would like. There are ways you can reduce the sense of alienation you may sometimes feel. There are specific things you can do to minimize your sense of distance from your daughter and maximize your sense of closeness.

How to Help Your Daughter Separate without Disconnecting

It's tricky to strike a balance between just the right amount of independence and dependence to allow teens. Ideally you want to remain involved without interfering, demonstrate your concern without restricting, and remain close without intruding. Too much interference and control may take the wind out of your daughter's sails. Your daughter needs some freedom in order to feel happy and proud. There are some ways you might help her to separate naturally without having to disconnect from you in the process.

What You Can Do

★ Give her plenty of opportunities for adult privileges, freedom, and decision-making when appropriate and with suitable supervision. Guide her, but let her run her own life as much as possible.

★ Take an interest in her activities and plans. You might say, "Tell me all about it. What's the plan? What do you get to do? What interests you the most about doing this?"

★ Encourage her when she makes plans apart from you. For example, "I'm so glad you get to do this. It sounds like so much fun."

★ Ask her if you can offer any help with planning, preparation, or transportation.

★ Ask her about her activities. For example: "What did you like about the party?" "Would you go again? Why or why not?" "What was the best part of your trip?" "What didn't you like?" "I'd love to hear what happened."

★ Demonstrate your faith in her ability to make responsible choices as she exercises her independence. Notice and point out examples to her.

★ Continue to plan mother/daughter time when it works. Don't stop being with her just because she is having more fun with friends or outside activities.

★ Encourage ongoing family outings in addition to her activities away from you. Your daughter may feel embarrassed at times doing things with the family because she's afraid she'll appear childish to others. Give her choices when you can, and when you can't, discuss the importance of your plans as a family together. Most girls end up having fun when they can be involved in the planning for such outings.

★ Have fun when you can be together and bring your sense of humor with you. For example, plan a day or evening that you can spend together doing something you both enjoy. Popular ideas include renting movies, taking a trip, sewing, planning a game night (invite another mom and daughter to join you), picking out your favorite CDs and dancing together, going to an exercise class or working out, walking the dog, eating popcorn, going shopping, shooting hoops, baking and decorating cookies or a cake, making a gingerbread house, playing tennis, working on a craft project, painting or redecorating her bedroom.

★ Treat her with the same respect you would another adult when you are listening to her ideas and plans. Don't treat her like a child.

★ Be someone she can talk to about what she wants to do. If you resist the urge to jump in and immediately deny her the opportunity to do or go somewhere, she will be more likely to want to share her ideas.

★ Listen, don't lecture. Try to understand her desire for independence. If you're talking more than she is, you may not be listening enough, which means you won't understand her either.

★ Continue to show your affection whether she accepts it or not.

★ Quit telling her what to do. It's better to let her learn how to be responsible. If you're helping her with something she is planning, make suggestions rather than demands.

★ Let the rope out slowly as she increases her independence from you, and gradually give her more freedom when she has shown she can use it responsibly.

★ Create a safe and stable home. Girls will retreat to their home base for advice and encouragement when acceptance and love are in plentiful supply.

★ Give her reason to be proud of you. Daughters like staying connected to their moms, especially when they can feel proud of them around their friends.

FREEDOM FROM A GIRL'S-EYE VIEW

Adolescent girls acknowledged both pros and cons to growing up. They said they especially like having more privileges and being able to go places without adults. They enjoy being trusted to manage their own time. Teen girls also acknowledged what's hard about growing more independent and the frustrations some feel at not having *more* freedom.

Straight Talk from Daughters

★ *You have to start making more of your own decisions, and they're decisions that can affect the rest of your life and that's kind of scary.*

★ *I'm told to do more chores, so I hate having more responsibilities than I used to. If I want more freedom, I have to work for it. That sucks!*

★ *I want to get out and do things with my friends and I want more freedom than I get. I still can't drive, and that's annoying because I want to be out and doing things without adults always having to tag along.*

★ *I want more fun and more money! But I can't find a job yet.*

★ *Friends want me to do more things. I feel pressured, like, if I don't have permission to go do things without an adult, I'll be seen as uncool, and I'll lose friends, and that feels bad.*

★ *I still can't do everything I want. Like no R-rated movies and no car to drive. It holds me back from life, you know?*

★ *R-rated movies? That's nothing. I do whatever I want. My mom doesn't have a clue about half the stuff I do. What she doesn't know won't hurt her, or me, dude!*

The Importance of Trust

Accepting your daughter's independence does not mean accepting all of her behaviors. It also doesn't mean you should stop monitoring her activities and whereabouts. Balance your acceptance with control, to help guide her safely over the bridge to independence that she may be so eager to cross.

Your presence in your daughter's life remains just as important as it was in her younger years. Just because she's old enough to fend for herself, don't think you're not needed or wanted. The attachment between the two of you remains important to your daughter's mental health and well-being throughout her development. Set priorities with your time so that you aren't missing out on meeting your daughter's needs. It's important to remain as physically and emotionally available to her as you can.

If you have trouble trusting your daughter because of real or imagined behaviors in the past, ask yourself if you might not be worrying about your own behaviors at her age. If you feel guilty, anxious, and regretful about your own experiences growing up, you may be expecting the same behaviors from her. If your daughter has broken your trust, you might see if approaching her with a new attitude could influence her differently. If you haven't tried taking a positive approach to the notion of "letting her go," it could make a difference.

What You Can Do

★ Trust her. If you don't already, behave as if you do.

★ Expect her to do the right thing. If you expect the worst, you may get it.

★ Stay attached. She needs to feel loved at all times. Show her you're interested in what she's doing by paying attention to what she's doing!

★ Approve of her. Show her that you like her. Don't let yourself run low on emotional and moral support.

★ Give her the benefit of the doubt. Accusations breed mistrust.

★ Be flexible. Rigid mothers suffer more.

★ Be physically available. Always be ready to hang out with her when she gives you the opportunity to enter her space.

★ Accept the fact that she will make mistakes. Don't expect perfection or make it a requirement for your approval.

★ Practice the art of mother/daughter bonding (in other words, anything you have fun doing together).

★ Practice "letting her go" when it's easy to. The bigger decisions will be less overwhelming when you've been working up to them gradually. (The Stretching Exercises at the end of this chapter can help you get started.)

★ Let her exercise independence while you exercise acceptance.

PRIVATE LIVES: COPING WITH HER TIME AND SPACE

It's one thing to be kicked out of the department store dressing room or a bathroom. It's another when your daughter informs you that you're not welcome to enter her bedroom or, worse yet, slams the door in your face. How much privacy does a girl need? How much privacy do you need? Whatever your answer, your daughter probably needs more.

Striking a Balance between Privacy and Safety

Your daughter may need a lot of privacy and space, but that doesn't mean it should be at the expense of your relationship or her safety. It's important to strike a balance on this issue.

Time away from you to visit with friends gives your daughter the opportunity to socialize with peers and learn about the new intimacy of friendship. Your daughter also needs time alone in her own world without anyone to relate to but herself. Part of an adolescent girl's development includes learning how to be by herself.

Private time and space gives her time to reflect, relax, plan, dream, and, as my daughter puts it, "chill out." Growing up takes an enormous amount of energy, and your daughter needs the opportunity to personally refuel.

A seventeen-year-old girl talked about privacy this way:

> When you reach a certain age, you begin to want more privacy, and it's kind of a difficult time for you and your mom because you have to learn how to deal with not having her in your life as much. She has to deal with not being wanted, like, I mean, you want her, but you just don't want her knowing everything anymore. When we were little, we didn't try to be private at all. Now as we grow up, it's totally different.

It's important to allow your daughter privacy so that she can learn to take care of herself and become comfortable in her own company. The onset of menstruation for many is the catalyst for privacy needs. The ways you respect your daughter's desire for privacy teaches her how to respect her own, and *yours*. But there are also appropriate times to intervene and sometimes interrupt her privacy "rights."

What You Can Say

★ "Privacy is an important need."

★ "I want you to have privacy and I want you to know I will still monitor your activities when online, visiting with friends, or watching movies, etc."

★ "Your room is your own, but I reserve the right to have access to your space if I ever have reason to be concerned about your safety or welfare."

★ "If you break the trust I have for you, you may be choosing to forfeit your privacy until trust can be rebuilt. This includes searching your room, computer, and notes for signs of danger or serious problems that may put you at risk."

★ "As long as we have an understanding of what my expectations are, you're free to protect your privacy and I'll respect your space, belongings, and personal time."

★ "I expect you to respect my privacy, too."

THE MOTHER CRITIC

Today, many mothers are striving to parent their teenage daughters differently. They want to practice more openness, engage in ongoing discussions, and try to keep the lines of communication untangled. This doesn't seem to change the fact, however, that daughters are still changing in ways mothers can't always understand or predict. Teenage girls seem to live by rules that are inherent to their age. And sometimes they can be strangely, dramatically, and even accurately critical of you.

It's not easy to emulate Mother Teresa when you're raising a teenage daughter. Mothers say they want to give love and support to their daughters but are often shut down in their attempts. This happens a lot when girls take a critical and negative stance against their mothers.

Adolescent girls almost universally seem to find fault with their mothers. The critical views they express hold their mothers at bay, perhaps as a way to set themselves apart and maybe in their own way to say, "I'm not you!" and "I want to be me."

Straight Talk from Moms

★ *Most days my daughter can't wait to get away from me. She's critical of my every move and complains that I'm "embarrassing." I honestly don't know what I've done when she tells me this. She wants to be alone or with her friends. She acts like she hates me! And I think she really does.*

★ *It wouldn't be so bad if she didn't sound like she liked criticizing me so much. Why do they enjoy it so much?*

★ *My daughter is fine when we're alone. She gets snotty when her friends are around. It's like she's trying to prove to them she doesn't need a "mommy" and doesn't want to look like a baby in front of them.*

★ *I'm the mom. Apparently that means I'm supposed to be able to take whatever my daughter dishes out, like I must have a core of steel and an "S" on my chest for "super self-esteem."*

★ *No matter how bad it gets (if I can help it), I try not to take her comments personally, even when she's picking me apart with no regard for my feelings. But there are days when I feel fragile too, you know? When I've had enough, she hears about it!*

★ *My daughter has become the ultimate "mother critic." As she's grown more independent, she's become unbearably sensitive about how I look, what I say, what I do, what I wear, how much my gray hair is showing, and she obsesses about whether or not I'm going to embarrass her for any reason that day. I never felt old until I hit this stage. Now I'm under the microscope and under her constant scrutiny.*

✱   *It's not so bad for me, because as the older one has snubbed me, the younger one sees it as an opportunity to grow closer to me. She has a chance to have me all to herself while the other one is taking every chance she can to get away from me. It helps me remember I'm not all bad and not take the older one's rejection so personally. It's been good to be able to grow closer to my younger daughter in the process.*

✱   *All I hear is, "You wear your pants too high, Mom. They are so weird looking, Mom. Pull them down around your hips, you look so geeky!" And then when I do happen to buy a pair of jeans that fall at my hips, she'll say, "Don't you think you're a little too old to be dressing young like me?" I can't win. She makes sure I can't win! What's that about?*

She Tells It Like She Sees It

Your daughter may have some valid gripes, but keep in mind that, more often than not, she is projecting her own feelings of insecurity and sometimes self-hate onto you. She may really be demonstrating the sense of painful frustration she feels about herself. Hopefully, by being aware of this, you can learn to respond to her hurt and pain, and less to your own. On the other hand, she may just be "telling it like it is" because she hasn't learned any other tactful way to say it to you yet.

Many of the girls I spoke with said they saw their critiques as constructive and helpful to their mothers. "It's for her own good," one teen told me. "I try to help her look less weird."

I shared my own story with a group of mothers discussing the critics in their homes. Here's what I told them:

When my own daughter was six years old, she asked about a beauty pageant she saw on television one night. I tried to explain what it was and then added in jest that I had been in a pageant myself once, but had declined the crown because it went against my beliefs. She looked up at me in startled amazement and said, "You could have won, Mommy. You look just like my Barbie!" It's hard to believe that the same dear, sweet child who made that remark is now a full-blown adolescent who recently compared me to a woman in an ad for a bladder-control product.

I also had to threaten to cut her off from ice cream blizzards if she ever disclosed the highly confidential details of a trip we took to an outlet store. We were shopping for bathing suits. For what seemed like weeks afterward, she would lie in bed at night laughing about it. "Not funny!" I had to keep shouting through her door. She said it was the flashbacks she kept seeing in her mind that were so hysterical. She politely explained it was the mental image of me in "that one bathing suit" that was stuck in her head—the one she bribed me to try on, "just in case it would turn out to be really flattering," she had said.

I knew better than to believe that line, but she was so convincing I thought it might be possible. Anyway, I tried the thing on and we both laughed ourselves sick. I admit it was truly a hysterical moment. But I've decided to move on with my life and she was still laughing about it!

One night I decided to set the record straight. I told her she was mistaken. I explained that the shopping trip was not funny, not even a bit funny. In fact there was nothing funny about it! I added that surely it was not something anyone would find humorous for the rest of their lives. Before she could finish saying, "Okay, Mom," she went into another uncontrollable spasm. Trying to salvage some shred of my dignity, I made the mistake of telling her proudly, in my most self-important voice, "There was a time when you thought I could be a beauty queen, and I looked like your Barbie doll, you said." In the time it took me to blink once, she retorted, "In your dreams, Mom! I *so* never said that!"

Moms have to be tough at times like this. Your ego will take a beating if you aren't careful. Take some basic steps to protect yourself when your daughter goes into a hypercritical mode.

What to Do Under Attack

★ Defend yourself by pointing out and exaggerating all your good qualities.

★ Tell her stories from your past that make you look really good.

★ Laugh along like you think it's funny too, and then call your best friend and commiserate about how unfair and inaccurate teenage perceptions are.

★ Tell her to "give it a rest."

★ Give her a taste of her own medicine and jokingly pout awhile.

★ Never try any article of clothing on that your daughter says, "Trust me, Mom, just try it, I think you could look really great in this."

★ Remember, on good days you're as young as you feel.

★ Remember, bad days never accurately reflect your age.

★ Remember that someday she may too have a daughter. What goes around comes around for all of us.

★ Consider apologizing to your own mom for giving her the same treatment when you were a teenager.

It would seem that "mother critics" arise from the desire for newfound independence. Even though there's nothing new about it, this is the part of parenting adolescent daughters that probably feels like new territory to every generation of parents that comes along. It's the nature of the beast, so to speak.

I LOVE YOU WHEN I NEED YOU

Your daughter is likely to vacillate between her desire for independence and her need to remain dependent. At times when she is striving the hardest to be independent, she may end up being the most dependent on you. Mothers are often confused and feel inadequate when they can't always adjust quickly enough to the changing needs of their daughters. Both moms and daughters express ambivalence about this perplexing time.

Straight Talk from Moms

★ *It's confusing. Sometimes she has her favorite stuffed animal and she's cuddling with me on the sofa and she's my baby again. Other times I can see her totally close off physically from me. She's growing away from the physical touch and comforting that I have always loved to give.*

★ *Sometimes my daughter still calls to me to come kiss her good night. I tuck her into bed and may sit with her for a while. That can happen on the same day she bolted away from me on the couch, annoyed, because I sat too close to her.*

★ *I miss my adoring, cuddly little girl who use to think the sun rose and set in my eyes, especially when she gets that tone in her voice. You know the one they use when you're trying to help with homework and she says something like, "You just don't get it!" She can turn on me just like that!*

★ *They only want us on their terms now. It's the "I love you when I need you, but leave me alone when I hate you" syndrome.*

Straight Talk from Daughters

★ *Sometimes I don't want my mom around. I want more independence from her. Usually I'm fine with it, but sometimes there's just things you don't want to share with your mom or anybody. I guess we're a little less open and close than we used to be, but I still want to be close.*

★ *Instead of us running up to our moms for hugs and kisses, now our moms run up to us for hugs and kisses! I hate that. But I still like it when she wants to tuck me in bed and kiss me good night.*

★ *When I'm feeling afraid or nervous, I want my mom more. But hey, when things are going okay, leave me alone, sometimes!*

TRUE FEELINGS MEAN MORE

The mothers I spoke with told me they worried a lot about the ways their daughters perceived them. Regardless of how emotionally secure and intact their own self-esteem normally was, when they felt their daughters pulling away from them, most mothers wrestled with a sense of insecurity about their changing role. They worried about questions like: I wonder how wonderful or terrible she makes me sound to her friends? Does she wish she had a different mom, now? Does she harbor a grudge for all the mistakes I've made? Would she say something to others that would surprise me if I were to know? What does she really feel about me? What will it be today, "Loves me or loves me not?" How can I be a better mom to her? What should I be doing differently in this emotionally challenging stage of her development?

Who better to ask than their daughters?

I admit, I expected to hear more complaints. I was prepared for the possibility of severe mother-bashing sessions. I expected to hear about all the things daughters thought their mothers were doing wrong. What I overwhelmingly heard from these girls, however, was a very different story. Despite the occasional critical moods they admitted to succumbing to at times, girls between the ages of eleven and eighteen told me they not only liked their moms but also admired and respected them. At a time when increased independence was happening for all of them, they told me what they wanted the most from their moms was *more* time with them, not less. They told me they usually *loved* being with their mothers.

Straight Talk from Daughters

★   *Our mothers shouldn't always believe what we say or how we act. True feelings mean more.*

★   *We still love our mothers, but it's just in a new way. We're different and we can't stay the same little girl or kid they had. Now we like the closeness in a more grown-up way.*

★   *I want her to spend more time with me.*

★   *I want to have more fun together.*

★   *I want to do things with her!*

★   *I'm getting to know my mom better than when I was younger.*

★   *Just being together and having fun is what's important to me.*

★   *I like and respect my mom.*

★   *I care about my mom's opinions of me.*

★   *I want my mom to be proud of me because I care about what she thinks.*

★   *I wish my mom could be around more. I miss her a lot.*

ON THE ROAD TO INDEPENDENCE

Accepting your daughter's desire for independence is accepting the fact that she's developing in a healthy way. Your attitude and approach to her journey can positively influence her feelings of confidence and anticipation as she begins.

A Guiding Light

There are a number of important ideas to consider as you prepare to guide your daughter toward greater independence. Your acceptance and enthusiasm are essential. Remember, your daughter needs you more than ever. Contrary to what her behavior may indicate, never forget this for a moment.

What You Can Do

★ Transform your bond in order to maintain it. Be open and willing to grow in new ways with your daughter.

★ Embrace change. Don't fear or fight it. If you deny change, you may miss out on new and different opportunities for closeness and may lose the chance to build new memories at this stage. Change can bring you closer together.

★ Reframe your daughter's acts of independence, rejection, or rebellion as an attempt to influence your understanding of her. She needs to renegotiate, not terminate, your relationship.

★ Believe in the value and importance of your daughter's independence. To help you identify specifics, make a list of what is (or might be) good about having an independent daughter. For example, it might include:

1. She can think for herself under pressure.

2. She will adjust to college life more easily.

3. She can take care of herself in new situations.

★ Tell your daughter directly what you like about her desire for independence. You might say, "I think it's great that you have the ability to think for yourself." "I like the fact that you can act on your own behalf when you need to." "I'm glad you enjoy the excitement of change and adventure in your life." "Your sense of independence will help you lead a full and happy life." "Personal freedom is a good thing. Your growing maturity will help you use it wisely." "Your growing independence is a healthy sign that you're comfortable with yourself."

★ Be honest about the conflict inside you if it's hard to accept her independence. You might explain, "I know it's natural for you to want to do more on your own now, but sometimes I need extra time to adjust to it."

★ Prepare her for times when she will not be able to exercise her independence. You might say, "Even though you're old enough to do a lot more on your own, I won't always approve of every situation you want to be a part of." "I want to support you, but there will be times I need to think things through a little longer, and my answer won't always be yes."

★ Every time you approve or disapprove of a particular situation requiring a sense of independence, explain your reasons why. You might say, "It sounds like you've made plans that will be fun and safe." "I like that you've taken the responsibility to explain where you'll be, with whom, and how you'll take care of yourself." "Thanks for explaining the details of your plans. You've showed me what good judgment you have about doing this on your own." Or, if you disapprove: "I don't know enough about your friends to let you attend this party." "I'm not willing to give you permission to go out on a school night." "I'm not ready to say 'yes' in this situation. There are too many unknowns."

★ Use humor when you can. You might say, "No! Don't leave me! I'm nothing without you!" "Your independence helps me a lot. *You* can make the French toast this morning." "I don't want you to grow up right now, so you'll have to put it off another day."

★ The best way to inspire your daughter's independence is to demonstrate your own. Girls need to see their moms as women with their own needs and desires. If you believe exercising your independence is a way to fulfill your greatest potential, she will, too.

★ Help your daughter understand that healthy independence is a combination of independence *and* dependence. A balance between the two usually benefits people the most. Explain that girls can practice too much independence when they stop needing others and try to tackle everything in life by themselves. A certain amount of dependence on others is important to continual growth and development.

★ Prepare to feel rejected sometimes. Make a decision not to take it personally. If you do take it personally, tell her why. How you handle your rejection will help your daughter learn how to handle rejection when it happens to her.

When Girls Fear Their Independence

Some girls find it difficult to exercise their independence and may not be comfortable functioning alone or without you. There could be any number of reasons why your daughter doesn't feel ready to seek new freedoms. If she is maturing at a slower rate, she simply may not be ready; she doesn't feel the need for increased independence yet. The best course of action is to relax and take the pressure off her. Encourage her and let her know you are confident she will be ready to take on more freedom, given a little more time.

If your daughter has suffered a trauma of any kind, it is likely that she will be more dependent. She may also be suffering from anxiety or fears that are troublesome enough to prevent her from taking the risk of becoming more independent. Another possibility is that your family and home environment may not encourage independence. In any case, the best thing you can do for your daughter in these circumstances is to seek outside support. A professional counselor or therapist can assess what difficulties may be contributing to your daughter's reluctance to spread her wings. A counselor or therapist who your daughter likes can be a tremendous benefit to her. Having an ally who will listen and offer useful coping skills can prevent future problems and needless suffering.

SO WHAT IF IT'S NOT THE WAY IT USED TO BE?

There are some moments you remember forever. Every now and then you get a little glimpse back into the past and pine for the way it used to be with your daughter. And sometimes she still responds to you in ways she did when she was younger.

Here's what happened to me. I took my thirteen-year-old daughter to school one morning before I was to leave for San Diego on a business trip. "I'll be home in six days, honey, and I'll miss you desperately every day," I told her. In the automatic pilot voice of a teenager, she responded, "Okay, I will miss you, too." It didn't take my skills as a trained therapist to hear the dull, lifeless quality in that comeback.

Then, sitting in the car, I momentarily reflected on how it used to be: "Hug and kiss!" she would insist. "Hug and kiss! Hurry home *fast*, Mommy! I'll be waiting and *waiting* for you, so hurry!" Even at the age of five, she had a grip so strong that it left my neck aching.

We had a strict ritual we followed every time we parted. One morning, I was distracted and drove away without waving to her. When I suddenly realized I had forgotten, I slammed on the brakes and backpedaled a block or so. When I arrived at the house, I saw her nose pressed flat against the window, where she dutifully stood for every coming and going. I saw her head bounce up and yell to my husband, "She's back!" We waved and blew kisses as I pulled away again. This time, she came running out in her favorite cartoon pajamas and sprinted down the sidewalk waving like people do at a ship being launched out to sea. My eyes strained to see her image in my rearview mirror as I rounded the corner. And that's the way it used to be when I ran to the store without her. That's the way it was whenever we separated.

But what did I expect now, sitting in the car at her school, in front of 500 teenagers milling about? Certainly not that kind of display. I could let it go. And then she turned to me, and said, "No really, Mom, I will miss you. I'm just not going to show it." As she navigated her backpack out the car door she flashed me the same big smile I have memorized. Our eyes met for an instant and connected in the same way they have for thirteen years, and I replied, "I completely understand. I really, really do." And I really did. "Love you," she said. "Love you more," I replied and I drove away, content, knowing all the feelings we held had been expressed.

We found a new way to do what we've always done. It was another beginning and ending in the life of our relationship. I hadn't lost a thing. We had simply found a new way.

STRETCHING EXERCISES

To help your daughter grow in her independence, and to help you grow in your acceptance, pick and choose from the following exercises designed to help you begin to safely "let go."

Exercise: Practice Independence

★ When eating out, ask your daughter if she and a friend want to sit at their own table and order separately from you.

★ Practice going your separate ways at museums, shopping trips, and movies. Establish meeting times and places and a plan for the unexpected.

★ Let your daughter run some errands for you with or without a friend.

★ Put your daughter in charge while you are away on a trip.

Exercise: Imagine Independence

Try having one of the following conversations while you're driving in the car or sitting down for a meal together:

★ Ask your daughter where she would go if she could travel to any place in the world. Who would she go with and why? Would she want to travel alone? Why or why not? How long would she want to be gone? What would her plans and goals be for this particular trip? What would be the pros and cons of going at her current age or of waiting until she is older?

★ Ask your daughter how she would spend one week being completely alone. Ask her where she would go and what she would do.

★ Ask your daughter how she would design her own apartment or home. Ask her to describe what it would look like.

Exercise: Develop Independence

Encourage your daughter to develop new skills that promote her sense of independence. For example, you might encourage her to attend a baby-sitting course, first-aid instruction, self-defense class, outdoor challenge course, wilderness retreat, camp, or organized trip.

CHAPTER 2

Conflict and Power Struggles

I used to be able to reason with my daughter. I mean she wouldn't always like it when I told her she couldn't do or have something, but I could explain my decision, and she'd respectfully say, "Oh. Okay, Mom." Now that she's a teenager, it's like having a two-year-old again. She's so demanding. Last week she saw something she wanted me to get her and said, "I want this! I need it! You need to take me there to get it now!" I explained in a reasonable way why I couldn't agree to her demand. But she said again, "But I want it. You just don't understand. I need it." I calmly and intelligently gave her an explanation for my reasoning, but she continued to hammer away at me about it. She dramatically insisted that I just didn't understand the depths of her need. After several more attempts of trying to discuss it in an adult-like fashion, I got so frustrated that the next time "I want it!" came flying out of her mouth I completely lost my cool and just screamed back, "You can't have it! So there!"

—Mother of a thirteen-year-old daughter

Autonomy and conflict seem to go hand in hand. Your daughter is growing in her ability to think, reason, and form her own opinions.

She has a lot of powerful drives and desires that she wants to fulfill and control. Delayed gratification might be hard for her to accept willingly. And if she can't quickly gain the power and control she wants, she may argue or wage a full battle against you in an attempt to gain it.

Adolescent girls are often wise beyond their years one moment and childish the next. Their thinking can be unpredictable. However, at times, mothers can be unpredictable, too. Under just the right pressure and strain, even the most rational, calm, and skilled communicator can unexpectedly regress. Mothers often admit they say and do things they wouldn't normally do when arguments erupt with their teenage daughters. Though it may not always be intentional on your daughter's part, it's probably safe to say she knows your "breaking point."

If and when you reach your breaking point, remember this: Conflict is common and necessary during the teen years. It even has benefits. In the long run, when conflict can be constructively expressed and resolved, it can help your daughter, as well as your relationship, grow and mature.

THE PRINCESS SYNDROME

Teens tend to be extremely egocentric, especially during the early and middle phases of adolescence. They can be consumed by self-centeredness. Endless streams of self-focused questions may fill their minds and at times it may be almost impossible for most girls to consider the needs of others above their own. Consequently, they are frequently accused of being self-seeking, demanding, and defiant. As one mother put it, "They seem only to care about themselves; my daughter thinks she's royalty and expects me to be her maid!" This period of development is often mistaken for selfishness, but a closer look at the "princess syndrome" reveals more than meets the eye.

Teenage girls go through a period of feeling "exposed" and uncomfortable living in the social world. It's common for them to feel noticed, judged, and under public scrutiny. They may feel like they're on stage wherever they go, believing that others are intently interested in them and their behavior. Self-consciousness causes most girls to feel highly sensitive to real or anticipated criticism and to the opinions of others. They are quick to criticize others in the same way they feel others are criticizing them. When adolescent girls become self-critical, they may act superior and egocentric to compensate for their own feelings of inadequacy. This acute sense of self-consciousness prevents them from being able to totally relax in the world.

It is genuinely hard for teenage girls to think rationally about themselves and their experiences. Teens see themselves as unique and more socially significant than they really are. Girls often tell me, "I'm the only one who feels this way," "I'm probably the only one whoever told you this," or "I know I'm the only one who ever had this happen."

A fifteen-year-old described an embarrassing moment that resulted in a "fight" with her mom: "I was invited to a guy's party and my mom had to call his parents just because she didn't know him. It was so embarrassing. Nobody else has to do that. I looked like such a baby! I think I'm old enough to do things without my 'mommy' calling my 'little friends' parents, you know?"

When this teenager finished sharing the above experience with a group of eight girls, all of them said that their parents made calls like that, too. They were all surprised when they learned they weren't the only ones with parents who "made them look bad in front of friends and guys."

During this time in their lives, teens have a hard time taking in rational explanations and potentially helpful feedback that is offered to them. Your daughter is more likely to discount your responses as being irrelevant and meaningless, often escalating conflicts between you. Your daughter's self-perceptions may be accurate at times and inaccurate at other times. Knowing this can help you cope, not give in, to her demands.

If nothing else, you may be able to find some humor in witnessing your daughter's melodramatic concerns. Of course, this doesn't mean laughing at her, but rather appreciating how hard it is for her to think any other way. The truth is, mothers can't help but find some situations funny. And that's as it should be. When humor isn't used against your daughter, enjoy it when you can.

The following story from a mother provides a good example:

My sixteen-year-old daughter and I were on a weekend vacation at the beach. We had just returned to our motel when I heard her suddenly holler, "What? You didn't pack a blow-dryer? You should have known!" I told her, "It's okay, our hair will dry fast in this hot weather." "But we need to leave now!" she whined. "It's okay; it'll dry fast," I told her again. "But my hair is soaking wet, Mom!" "Honey," I said, "it's summer. We're driving home in the car. Who cares what we look like?" "Well, maybe I care! You're already married!"

Now I was completely mystified. I asked her, "Are you expecting to meet your future husband driving home on the freeway today?" "Yeah, right," she said, with an exasperated scowl that suggested I understood nothing. "People can see in our car, Mom! They'll see me and think, 'She'll never find a boyfriend looking like that!'"

Here's what I've been through with my fourteen-year-old daughter:

> I was rolling the shopping cart down the center aisle of the grocery store when my daughter suddenly turned toward me in a state of absolute panic and screeched under her breath, "Mom!" I jumped, thinking we were about to be attacked. "What is it?" I asked, searching frantically around us. She silently took control of the shopping cart from me. "Mom, do you realize how slow you are pushing this cart?" "What's the hurry?" I asked. "Mom! Do you realize you're in the middle of the store?" "Yes, I do, why?" "Mom! Do you realize we're going to have to backtrack down every aisle, because you started here? It's a total waste of time shopping like this." I wanted to attack, but kept my cool. She continued, "People can't even get past you, you go so slow!" I was getting angry: "Like who? There's not another soul in sight!" Not satisfied, she went on, "Mom! You did almost run into someone back there!" I ignored her until we reached the meat department. I picked up a tongue that looked like it used to belong to a very large animal. Before I knew what it was, I asked sarcastically, "What in the world is this thing and why is it next to food?" She started again. "Mom! Everyone can hear you!" Just as sarcastically I replied, "Well, unless they secretly hooked me up to the store intercom, hon, I doubt it!" "Don't call me 'hon,'" she said in disgust. "And don't sing and dance with the store music! You look really, really weird. I know people here, you know." "Okay," I said. "let me get this straight. Don't sing, don't push, don't talk, don't dance, don't move, is that right?" "Basically," she responded.

We loaded our car with groceries and before our seatbelts were fastened into place, my daughter changed the radio station, turned up the music, started singing off-key and suggested we go rent movies, bake cookies, and have a "girls' night" together. I stopped the car and said, "I'm confused. Thirty seconds ago you had me on parole. Now you want to be with me?" "Well sure!" she chirped happily. "we won't be in public. I don't care what you do at home!"

The princess has unpredictable thinking and an unpredictable use of logic. It comes and goes. Mothers are often dumbfounded by it all and begin to wonder about themselves. "Am I crazy, or is she?"

You aren't, and she isn't. It's simply adolescent thinking at its best and most humorous.

MOTHER SUPERIOR

Teenage girls may act like princesses, but mothers can act like entitled royalty, too. Sometimes they even impose themselves on their daughters. You may believe you have the right, ability, and obligation to do so, but holding an attitude of superiority over your daughter is likely to escalate conflict to a more troublesome degree.

Mother "superiors" tend to measure everything their daughters say and do. They often contradict their daughter's thoughts and feelings if there is a disagreement. It's important to make the effort to not take exception to what your daughter says, just because it doesn't fit your views or standards. You may find it threatening when your daughter challenges you, but if you rebuff your daughter in ways that imply that her ideas are stupid or bothersome, you risk harming her self-esteem. What often results is resentful rage or withdrawal into depression.

Know-it-all moms may know a lot, but their daughters will never have the opportunity to benefit from them. What they are likely to learn are better skills for verbal duels, where winning is everything and power must be attained through battle. They may also learn that it's easier to withdraw into silence. If you disagree with your daughter, disagree, but don't contradict her. If you go against everything she says, you will discount your daughter's feelings and possibly take away her confidence.

Truly superior mothers are loyal to their daughters. They are able to hold their daughters' confidences. Girls need to be able to trust their mothers. A mother sees, speaks, and hears no evil toward her daughter. Being loyal means being faithful, steadfast, trustworthy, reliable, and devoted, and dedicated to the relationship you share. If you are genuine with her, you will live your life the way you talk and encourage her to do the same. You will build her up, not tear her down.

JUST A LITTLE R-E-S-P-E-C-T

Girls want and need respect, and they pay attention to who gives it to them. When you infuse your relationship with respect, you send a powerful message. Respect communicates a sense of reverence and admiration. It tells your daughter that you hold a high opinion of her.

When your daughter knows that the most important thing to you is preserving a happy relationship with her, it's easier to confront disagreements. If she knows, even in the midst of quarreling, that your ultimate goal is a good relationship, your daughter may be more willing to work through her feelings with you in a positive and respectful way.

Stressing the importance of your relationship communicates that your intent is not to blame, criticize, or win an argument. It says that you are not concerned with who caused the problem, but rather that it's important to you that the problem be solved. Finally, when you respect her feelings you are encouraging her to respect yours.

IT STARTS WITH COMMUNICATION

Many women feel so exhausted and frustrated by their thwarted attempts to communicate with their daughters that they give up trying. One mother told me she thought all the girls I would be speaking to would say the same thing. She told me: "The girls are probably all going to say, 'Oh, our mothers, they all talk so much! All they want to do is communicate!' I don't think they're even listening to us. They're just looking at our moles."

Mothers complain that their daughters don't want to listen to them. Girls complain that their mothers "don't understand." Girls hate lectures and being talked to like a baby. All of these attitudes and perceptions create conflict. However, just as problems are a part of life, conflict is a normal part of communication. It's not the conflict that can be so problematic; it's your reactions to conflict that usually create difficulties.

Communication is the key to preventing *or* encouraging conflict and power struggles. How you communicate will determine whether conflict leads to a healthy and helpful resolution or only serves to alienate you further from your daughter. Children and teens are especially sensitive to communication because so much of who they are becoming depends on what they hear from others.

Good communication is an art. It has to be developed. When communication is positive, it prevents conflict and power struggles. This chapter will introduce you to the key components of good, or positive, communication. Use it as much as you can. Bad communication encourages conflict. It builds tension and resentments. All parents fall victim to it sometimes. Avoid it as much as humanly possible. Ugly communication has the power to destroy relationships and people. It is psychologically manipulative and abusive, and it attacks a girl's self-esteem. Make the decision to refuse to go there.

Adolescent girls (especially those with counselor moms) tell me, "Too much talk about feelings gets sickening." They also tell me they know how to tune out there mothers when they get too boring. And yes, they admit, they notice the moles and bumps and wrinkles on your face, especially when you're not saying anything particularly interesting to them.

Teenage girls have also confided in me, however, that they feel unhappy when they are alienated and isolated from their mothers. Reliable and positive communication is absolutely imperative for girls as they progress through adolescence because it provides them with something they can depend on: a relationship with you.

Straight Talk from Daughters

★ *Sometimes I don't feel like I can tell my mom stuff. When I was little I shared everything. At this age it's more awkward.*

★ *I don't think most of us can talk to our moms. Girls who smoke or are into sex are going through a lot of things that they don't feel they can talk to their moms about.*

★ *Most moms I know are not easy to talk to.*

★ *I can't talk to my mom. I'm insecure about what she will think and worried that what I say to her will be wrong.*

★ *I get teased about what I say to my mom sometimes. I'm not sure how she's going to react, so I don't tell her anything.*

★ *I can't talk to my mom when she's, like, in a daze and stuff, and is in a really bad mood.*

★ *Girls who can talk to their moms have moms who encourage them to talk.*

★ *Some moms don't really care that much. My mom always tells me, "If you need to tell me something, you can. You don't have to, but you can." It's cool. I personally can talk to my mom.*

★ *If she's distracted, she usually won't listen to me. Why bother?*

★ *One way I get my mom's attention is to tell her I'm going down the street to get my nose pierced in ten places. Then she'll say, like, "What?" and then she'll listen.*

★ *Poke them! Sometimes you have to physically get their attention. It works!*

✦   *I yell at her when she's reading and flag my hand over her book or paper. Then she gets mad, but at least she's tuned in to me at that point.*

✦   *Everything I say is wrong, so why say anything at all?*

✦   *My mom does all the talking. She's the one who knows everything, and supposedly I'm too young to know anything. I hate talking to her.*

✦   *I think my mom's more like a friend now, like a close friend. Whenever I have trouble with anything, she'll just talk it over with me like a friend.*

✦   *My mom discusses things with me. She says, "This is right, this is wrong, and you need to decide what to do." She gives me more responsibility to take care of myself.*

To Listen to Me Is to Care about Me

One of the most common phrases a mother is likely to hear from her teenage daughter is "Listen to me!" Being listened to and feeling understood are important needs your daughter has.

Listening is one of the most important exercises in communication. Mothers are wise to practice it all the time. Listening is one of the best ways to communicate respect to your daughter. And it is not only the act of listening, but *how* you listen that communicates true feelings of respect.

It's easy to go on automatic pilot when responding to your daughter and to not really listen or hear her unique viewpoints about a situation or request. Good listening takes a great deal of concerted effort. It is not a passive or shallow activity. Rather, it requires you to focus all of your attention on your daughter. It means walking away from the computer, turning off the television or music, putting your reading material down, and making direct eye contact with her.

Listening is hard work sometimes because there is so much more to attend to than just the words being spoken. You must also pay attention to body language, voice tone, and inflections. When she says one thing but appears to really feel a different way, it's wise to explore that with her. Pointing out the incongruity between your daughter's words and behaviors can help her gain greater awareness about her true feelings and deepest needs.

How to Help Her Communicate

You can help your daughter communicate her feelings and needs by giving her encouraging responses that gently challenge her to speak about herself in more depth. Try out some of the following ways of asking questions. (Note: Complete each phrase with something your daughter has just mentioned.)

★ "What I hear you say is . . ."

★ "You're feeling . . ."

★ "It seems to me that . . ."

★ "I wonder if . . ."

★ "It sounds like . . ."

★ "What if you . . ."

★ "Maybe you . . ."

★ "Perhaps you're feeling . . ."

★ "What did you make of that when . . ."

★ "What might help you when . . ."

If you are listening effectively, you are more likely to be tentative in your responses. It's best not to assume you know your daughter's feelings better than she does. It's important you check out your assumptions with her and be sure you truly do see her experience from her perspective. Most teens are more receptive to input from their moms when they feel truly understood.

What You Can Do

★ Use "I messages." When you begin by explaining your own experience you are taking responsibility for your own feelings, modeling for your daughter how she can do the same. Examples of "I messages" include: "I feel . . .", "I am feeling . . .", "I feel this . . . when . . . because . . ." Encourage her to begin her statements with "I" as she responds to you. It will take some practice, but if you can begin to introduce "I" statements into your discussions and arguments, you'll feel the difference.

★ Avoid statements that begin with "you." Such statements send an accusatory message, which escalates defensiveness. Problem solving is quickly buried under the power struggle that is likely to follow.

When conflict is inevitable, good listening and responding skills will help you get through it with less pain and suffering. If you believe you have truly listened to your daughter and have been able to reflect back to her what she has been saying to you, the next step is to be sure you have a genuine understanding of *her*. Ask yourself how well you really know and understand your daughter. It is important to not only understand what she tells you but also to really know and value who she is.

To Know Me Is to Love Me

"You just don't understand" is another familiar phrase cried out by many adolescent daughters. When girls don't feel understood, they feel hurt. Even more painful for daughter's is the perception that their mothers do not even *want* to understand them. Not feeling understood means not feeling cared about. This is an emotional time bomb just waiting for the right time and place to detonate. Anger is all too often the inevitable outcome of feeling hurt.

The mother of a fifteen-year-old daughter offered this advice:

> You have to know your child the way you know yourself. If your daughter can't effectively verbalize what she's going through, you have to be able to read her behavior. The clues can be so subtle. It seems to me you learn to do that by spending time with her. That focused time with her, doing what she wants to do, that's how you learn to read the subtle cues to her feelings.

Sometimes girls may avoid discussing things that they think will make their mothers feel uncomfortable or upset. If your daughter fears being punished, belittled, humiliated, laughed at, or lectured to, she may not talk to you and, instead, get poor guidance from another source. Keep an open-door policy on discussing any subject.

It's natural for your daughter to keep parts of her developing inner self separate and secret from you. There may be a great deal about her that you will never know, but chances are she would like to be able to tell you more. A fifteen-year-old girl said this:

> There are things I should probably tell my mom, but I don't. She knows as much as I'll let her know. I wish I could tell her more about my deepest feelings and ask questions sometimes. I just don't know how. I know she wants me too, but I just can't. I don't know why. Some days my mom's like my best friend and it's cool. Other days she just pisses me off and I feel like she doesn't understand a thing about me and never will.

To really know your daughter, you must risk communication that goes beyond the day-to-day clichés and facts. Sharing personal beliefs, ideas, and opinions with her is a way to build communication to a more intimate level. However, at this level, you also risk more conflict because your views about some of these issues are likely to be different. Communicating personal feelings may also make you each feel more vulnerable.

What can you do if your daughter is reluctant to share herself with you? First, it's important to make a commitment to improve your listening skills and understanding. Then you can begin to talk openly about what makes it difficult to talk and find some non-threatening ways to begin. A mother offered this advice:

> Get a journal. I bought one for myself and one for my daughter because we both like to write. It's one of the best ideas I've had. It's bonding time. If she doesn't want to talk, I just announce it's our "journaling time," and then all she wants to do is talk! So every time I want to talk, I just take out my journal. It's rare that we ever have the time to write anything in them.

Some of the warmest memories between mothers and daughters occur in spontaneous moments where both feel mutually in sync and understood. Being safe to share intimate feelings adds to the vibrancy and health of your relationship.

THE ANGER TRAP

As in most relationships, arguments between mothers and daughters may seem to erupt out of nowhere. You don't always see problems coming. Stress factors such as premenstrual syndrome, hunger, fatigue, and overscheduling certainly may make you both more vulnerable to heated arguments.

You may also be vulnerable to the pressure that comes when you have to switch roles almost instantaneously. One minute you may feel like you're your daughter's best friend, and the next you feel like her worst enemy. Try thinking of yourself as though you were playing a fictional stage role as the enemy. (It's a temporary act and someone has to play the part.) While it's important not to discount your daughter's anger, it's also important not to take it to heart and hold a grudge. Her feelings about you will pass quickly, and you need to be ready to make the transition back to a positive role when they do.

Most teenage daughters have a lot to say about what makes them angry.

Straight Talk from Daughters

★ *What really gets me mad is when my mom tells me what I do wrong. I get defensive. She doesn't understand. Most of the time she's right, but I don't want her to know it.*

★ *My mom and I fight about my stepdad. It creates tension between us.*

★ *My parents are enemies. I'm in the middle. I can't talk about it to my mom because it starts a fight between us.*

★ *No one takes me seriously!*

★ *We get in arguments when we're deciding what we're going to do. She doesn't think I spend enough time with her and feels hurt.*

★ *My mom doesn't follow through with what she says. She puts off her promises.*

★ *Sometimes it's just hard to be nice to my mom. I get grumpy. Anything makes me mad.*

★ *It really annoys me when my mom can't understand me. It's hard when I can't get through to her! She keeps punishing me instead of listening! It's frustrating.*

★ *She won't admit when she's wrong. She doesn't think she ever owes me an apology.*

Straight Talk from Mothers

★ *These are confusing times. I don't know my boundaries with my daughter. I'm dancing around her all the time. Her dad has to step in sometimes and say, "I think you two girls need to sit down and figure this out." At first, I'm like, "Hey! I'm the mother. Don't put me on her level!" But he's right, and that's exactly what we have to do.*

★ *I just say, "Let's agree to disagree," and come back to it later.*

★ *I let her blow off steam. Anything I try to say in that moment, she won't hear anyway.*

★ *I try to focus on what she's doing right and acknowledge it. I do my best to stay calm.*

★   *What I do is kind of follow her around the house and try to get her to talk. She may talk a little here, a little there, but I will bug her. It works! Sometimes I can get her to really open up.*

★   *We yell. Sometimes we both have tantrums and dissolve into tears. One night she followed me out to the car. I got in, rolled up the windows, and we just sat and yelled at each other. Then we calmed down and laughed at ourselves.*

★   *I just listen and listen and listen, even when I don't agree.*

★   *Our anger is "out there." It's a part of who we are. So is crying. We can't always even agree about why we yell and cry.*

★   *My daughter needs space at that point, so I just leave her alone. It's better that way. After we're done being hysterical, we try to talk about it.*

★   *Part of my difficulty is that I usually understand where she's coming from. Her anger is really coming from a logical place. I'd feel the same way! So, as a mom, I really feel I need to validate how she feels and I'm really glad my daughter is saying these things to me. I would've never said to my mom what she says to me. I'm glad she can trust me.*

★   *I'm the biggest problem. We get angry at each other because I don't want her to grow up too fast. She's my first. I've never been through it and I really want to slow her down. And she doesn't want to slow down. She wants to go out and do something all the time instead of maybe doing something at home that's interesting. I think I'm probably the biggest problem because I can't get past these feelings yet.*

★   *I see something's bothering her and I want to keep asking, "What's wrong?" And I can see she just wants to pull away. I have to go through this whole self-talk thing, telling myself, "It's okay. She needs her space. It's not about me."*

★   *When my daughter gets mad at me, I have to say to myself, "It's not a popularity contest. It's okay for her to be mad at me." I struggle inside myself when she pulls away.*

★   *We have times that I call "meltdowns." It gets crazy. So we take a break, go to our separate rooms, and then come back and talk about it. We have a clear understanding of how we affect each other.*

★   *You really have to pick your battles. Save your energy for the big stuff and decide to let the small stuff go.*

★   *I remember that ultimately I'm fighting for her, not against her.*

WORKING THROUGH CONFLICT

Problem-solving discussions, staying problem-focused, and resisting the exchange of negatively charged emotions are all strategies that can help you work through conflict. Whether it's a specific problem, argument, disagreement, or full-blown attack, teenage girls have some ideas of what helps them, too.

Straight Talk from Daughters

★ *When I'm angry, I just want to be left alone. I don't want my mom to come to my room right away. When that happens, I'll get really mad and then I'm in trouble again.*

★ *Moms get so anxious to "deal with it," "get over it," and "fix everything" that they don't give you enough space. If you're not ready to deal with it yet, it makes things worse.*

★ *When you feel better later and then come back out, and she's still fighting with you, then you can't get past it! She has to learn how to let it go, too.*

★ *When we both apologize, it gives us some closure, and then we can be happy again.*

★ *Sit down and talk. If there's nothing to talk about, moms shouldn't just assume we don't want to be with them. Play games or go out and do a sport or other physical activity together. Spend time and do something with us. That helps prevent fights.*

★ *I put a sign on my door to tell my mom when I don't want to talk and when I want to be left alone.*

★ *Tell mothers to pay attention to how we react to them. Respect our privacy and let us make our own decisions to take care of ourselves.*

★ *Moms should really communicate with us. The truth might hurt, but it's better than avoiding it. It's better to be straight-out with things.*

★ *The most important quality to me about my mom is that she loves me. Being loving helps us get through the bad stuff that happens between us.*

★ *Mothers need to lighten up. They worry too much and make a big deal out of things that are no big deal. If they lightened up, half the arguments wouldn't happen.*

★　*It's really important to let us know we're loved. Mothers need to support us in whatever we do. Mistakes shouldn't change that.*

★　*Mothers need to communicate more as a friend than a mother.*

★　*They need to let us know that what we're going through is not weird or different and that we aren't the only ones who blow up for no good reason.*

★　*Act on what you say. Let me know you're serious about what you're saying.*

★　*Keep reassuring me, even though I act like I don't believe you. Keep complimenting and reassuring me.*

★　*Everything my mom says I remember. She may not think I listen, or care, or agree, but really I am listening. I do take everything she says to heart a lot of times.*

★　*Constructive criticism lets you know they are really paying attention.*

★　*I may not want to hear my mom's advice, but I think she still needs to give it. She shouldn't give up. She should keep saying it and giving it.*

★　*I love it when my mom rewards me. Not with things, but even just telling me that what I did was really awesome. It's fun to make people happy and it helps me feel less angry.*

★　*Mothers need to relate to us like they would anyone they respect. Like, don't assume we have to be commanded.*

YOUR STYLE OF RELATING

The communication strategies you employ and the way you relate to your daughter will influence how well you both are able to work through conflict together. Answer the following questions about your style of relating to your daughter:

1. Are you positive and hopeful when you speak to your daughter? (Going in with a proactive and optimistic outlook about any problem or situation can make a difference in how much you will actually be able to achieve.)

2. Are you encouraging, respectful, and truthful? (Whatever it is you have to say, it's important to help your daughter hear it without destroying her sense of dignity or attacking her

self-esteem. Convey your message in an understandable and unthreatening way.)

3. Do you use appropriate timing? (It's true that timing is everything. Choose a time when you are both relaxed and able to focus on the issue[s] at hand.)

4. Are you gracious with your words? (If anyone happened to "listen in," they should not hear anything offensive or negative about your daughter.)

It's not realistic to expect complete harmony. Remember, the two of you are from different generations. It's not pleasant to live through periods of bickering and strain, no matter how temporary it may be. But keep in mind that it's natural for your daughter to test your authority while she is trying to assert herself.

Nothing's Set in Stone

There is always more than one way to approach your daughter. During conflict or heated debates, the more flexible you can be, the more likely you and your daughter will learn from each other. Taking a rigid stance short-circuits communication and stifles the chances you have to grow closer. Dogmatic positions also leave little room for humor to find its way into your discussions. Generally, when you or your daughter take a close-minded approach to a subject, defensiveness and resistance are the result.

Exercise: Rating Your Openness

As a mother, it is clearly in your own best interest to be open-minded and flexible. When you're not, life gets harder. On a scale of 1 to 5, where 1 is "never" and 5 is "always," assess how open-minded you are. Have your daughter rate you, too. Compare your responses and discuss the variances, if any.

How do you rate?

_____ I carefully consider and evaluate all new ideas my daughter presents to me.

_____ I check facts to be sure they are correct before I include them in what I have to say.

_____ I can change opinions when I learn new things.

_____ I am fair in my judgments and decisions

_____ I can admit when I am wrong.

_____ I am flexible and willing to change my mind when it's the right thing to do.

_____ I am able to take into account what others advise or counsel me to do.

_____ I seek out the opinions and perspectives that my daughter holds.

_____ I can acknowledge and praise my daughter when she corrects a mistake I've made.

_____ I am comfortable letting my daughter direct our discussions.

_____ I don't focus on my daughter's shortcomings.

_____ I have a close friend or partner who I can confide in and receive an unbiased evaluation of my responses and decisions toward my daughter.

_____ I can accept it when my daughter disagrees with me.

ACTIONS AND CONSEQUENCES

All adolescent girls need guidance and discipline. When your daughter shows disrespect toward you or others, it's important to address her behavior swiftly and set clear limits around what you will not accept from her and what the consequences will be for the choices she makes. Discipline is still a vital part of your daughter's development. No matter how mature your daughter may seem or sound, she still needs your guidance throughout her adolescence. Her future success and maturity depend on her ability to practice delayed gratification, self-control, and respect for others.

In her book *Reviving Ophelia*, Mary Pipher writes: "Our tendency to blame parents, especially mothers, for their children's problems has paralyzed many parents. They are so afraid of traumatizing their children that they cannot set clear and firm limits. They are so afraid of being dysfunctional that they stop functioning" (1994, 252).

In many cases teens are still learning how to regulate their emotions, and they need parents to set helpful parameters around their behavior. Some acting out, anger, and rebellion are normal and healthy for adolescents as they work through the process of becoming an independent person. Unless you are among the few women who live with daughters who have easy temperaments all the time, without some discipline there is likely to be a great deal of chaos in your home.

The need for discipline varies considerably from teen to teen and may even vary from day to day. Ongoing and successful negotiation with your daughter will tend to minimize conflict. Keep in mind that disciplinary action seems to be less needed in homes where there is ample opportunity for discussion to take place.

Talking to your daughter is the best measure you can take. However, if you communicate too strictly or too permissively, it probably won't be effective. It's important to find a balance in your parenting approach.

Mothers do best when they are not afraid to be firm. When you are practicing effective discipline, you are educating, exercising, and preparing your daughter to cope with whatever comes her way in life. You can help your daughter respond to you as an authority figure and, at the same time, help her respond to her own sense of responsibility. A fourteen-year-old girl put it this way: "I don't get disciplined in the same way I used to. I mean, I do get disciplined, but it's different now because we can actually talk, and we can relate to each other, and it makes it different, easier."

The Fourteen Do's and Don'ts of Discipline

1. Do show respect for your daughter's opinions, no matter how off the wall you may believe they are.

2. Do give your daughter time to express her feelings and point of view.

3. Do explain and give reasons for your decisions. Besides conveying respect, this can also help your daughter internalize ethical and moral principles.

4. Do regulate your daughter's behavior with rules and structure. Don't be afraid to set limits on her freedom and behavior. Creating limits and policies together usually elicits more reasonable attitudes and less resistance.

5. Do provide feedback that helps your daughter feel good about who she is, apart from what her behavior(s) may have been.

6. Do focus on the behaviors that she needs to take responsibility for changing and, if necessary, help her come up with ideas for changing them.

7. Do use natural and logical consequences that are directed toward your teen's actions, not toward her as a person. This will help stimulate responsible decision-making.

8. Do respect your daughter's sense of individuality. It's okay to influence her ideas, but this is different from trying to force her into a preconceived mold to fit your own desires. Respect her as an individual, even when you don't accept all her ideas.

9. Do be a friendly and watchful bystander, ready and willing to step forward when help is needed.

10. Do create a happy home environment filled with empathy, warmth, understanding, and friendliness. The best-adjusted girls grow up in happy, loving homes where it's pleasurable to spend time together.

11. Do care about teaching your daughter the difference between right and wrong. Your daughter is more apt to admire and respect the strength of your convictions, even when she may not agree, especially when they are communicated to her from a position of love and respect.

12. Don't be wishy-washy. Your daughter will only be confused if you are unable to be firm and consistent about where you stand and what you expect of her. Conflicting expectations breed confusion, insecurity, and rebellious behavior. Consistency is important to raising happy and less anxious teens.

13. Don't demand obedience through corporal or demeaning punishment. You are likely to provoke your daughter's anger, hostility, and acts of delinquency by taking a controlling position with her.

14. Don't immediately withdraw your trust or lose confidence in your daughter the first time she steps out of line. Try to limit punishment in a first-time situation. If you are too harsh before she's had a chance to learn from her behavior, you risk severing the lines of communication.

Minimize the Risks

Every mother must decide what she will and will not accept and tolerate. How you enforce and monitor your expectations and limits will be guided by the standards and values you have chosen to live by.

Mistakes are a part of life and your daughter cannot be perfect. But you can help minimize the risks while she's still under your protection. Soon enough, she'll be out in the world without you. Hopefully by then, she'll have the advantage of a nearly full mature self and will have more resources to cope with mistakes and poor judgment. For now, enjoy having her with you. You're packing her bags with more skills to take over the bridge into adulthood.

NEGOTIATION SKILLS 101: CLOTHES, MALLS, MAKEUP, AND MORE

The most common power struggles between mothers and daughters occur over the day-to-day details of life and habits of living, centering on issues related to self-discipline and self-control.

Critical comments you might make about your daughter's habits of daily living, such as her hair, messy room, dirty laundry, chores, habit of sleeping late on weekends, long telephone conversations, habit of wearing tight, skimpy, or torn clothing, are usually poorly tolerated by teenage girls. If your daughter's drive for independence is met only by your increasing control in these areas, you are likely to experience greater conflict. "Nagging" is an effective way to inspire more resistance. It's a sure way to push your daughter away and create a chasm between you.

How your daughter looks, where she is seen, whom she talks to, and how she lives all have an impact on her sense of value and self-worth. Her desires may seem extreme to you and her wants may appear equally frivolous. Every mother seems to worry about what limits are appropriate to set for her daughter and what should be allowed and not allowed.

There are no hard-and-fast rules about when or if to let your daughter pierce her ears, navel, or tongue, how many hours a week she should be allowed on the computer and telephone, and how much money is reasonable to give her.

Most mothers agree that the culture puts far too much pressure on girls to look and dress seductively. They worry that their daughters are being pushed to look more mature under increasing pressure to meet a cultural ideal and appeal to men before they are ready. Some of your daughter's requests for what she wants to do or the way she wants to look may be hard for you to swallow. And not all girls will ask; they will just do it or tell you what they plan to do. It's important to encourage your daughter to be herself, not someone or something she isn't, and sometimes you have to set limits. Your daughter, however, may not see it the same way. It's important, therefore, to keep an open mind about her requests and desires. Some requests may be out of the question, but others deserve careful consideration. Being open to whatever your daughter asks for is critical to teaching her how to listen and negotiate. Whether she wants to attend a wild party or to demand a nose ring, your negotiation skills will help you address any controversial issue that comes up.

General Guidelines

Negotiation is actually a simple process that you can work on. The following guidelines will help you get started.

Take it slow. Peace talks between countries take considerable time and patience. Peace talks between mothers and daughters do, too. Let the negotiations begin by simply opening up the issue for discussion. Be prepared to take your time. Slow the process down whenever you feel the need. Keep in mind that it is possible for your daughter to change her mind. What she desperately needs or wants today may be old hat tomorrow. Sometimes, impulsive decisions lead to later regret. A good decision or choice takes careful consideration and planning.

Don't feel guilty about limiting your daughter's freedom. Before you open up negotiations with your daughter, keep in mind the "freedom factor." Too much freedom can be overwhelming for your daughter, even when she says it's not. Use good judgment and common sense to help build safe fences around her development. During adolescence, too much freedom can be frightening and dangerous.

Understand what negotiation is and isn't. When you negotiate, you talk, discuss, consult, settle, cooperate, bargain, collaborate, and basically reach a deal. If done right, it's a process that can head off potential struggles with your teen. When you work together to resolve a difference of opinion, the results are usually beneficial for both of you. But, remember, negotiation isn't the same thing as giving in. And it doesn't mean you both have to agree with the outcome. It also doesn't necessarily mean you will give your approval. Negotiation means you are encouraging your daughter's participation in the decisions that affect her, but you will always have the final say.

Establish a list of your negotiable and nonnegotiable issues. Before you begin, determine where you draw the line for what you are willing to accept and what is off-limits for your consideration. For example, you may decide you are open to discussing the issue of body piercing with the possibility of approval, but not to the issue of smoking or drinking alcohol. You may agree to discuss the possibility of piercing some parts of the body but not others. You may be open to negotiating an allowance increase, but not without a way of fairly earning it. You must determine what is negotiable and what is nonnegotiable.

What issues are you willing to consult with your daughter about? Will you consider adjusting curfew times, increasing Internet access, allowing a change in style of makeup and clothes, driving privileges? Make a list, if it helps, to gain some clarity about where you can be flexible and where you can't. Make two columns, one titled *negotiable* (if a mutual agreement can be reached, I may negotiate on these items) and the other, *nonnegotiable* (these can be discussed, but you need to know I am not comfortable opening these up for changes).

Discuss your reasons. Your daughter may be disappointed, frustrated, or angry when she sees what is nonnegotiable for you. She may also agree with what's on your list. Even though nonnegotiable items are not likely to ever change, it's important to discuss them and give the reasons for your decisions. You may want to tell her that, if after this discussion, you find you were in error, you will be open to adjusting your decisions in *either* direction.

Be firm and confident. When you are strong in your parenting role, it will help your daughter gain in strength, too. When she knows you are firm and clear about the stands you take, she will be more likely to understand that she can rely on you to do what's best, even if she disagrees.

Don't get sidetracked. Don't go off on tangents that have nothing to do with the decision at hand. It only confuses the issue. Stay focused and make a commitment to the negotiation process you've agreed to participate in.

Be inclusive every step of the way. Successful negotiation means being inclusive every step of the way. You have the final decision, but your daughter can trust that her viewpoint will be listened to and understood. Most girls tell me that it is easier for them to accept "no" after they have been through a fair and respectful process like this.

Brainstorm with your daughter. Establish the relative importance of her wants or needs. Are they really needs, or are they preferences? For example, "I don't really *need* to have blue hair, but I would *prefer* it." Help her distinguish between the two. You could ask: What does she think would be a fair outcome for her and for you? Why? What are the short-term and long-term consequences for this decision? Are there risks? If so, what are they, and how would she handle them? What do you need to have happen in order for you to be comfortable with agreeing to her wants or needs? Be specific. Can your daughter accept and meet those requirements for you? Are there any safety concerns about what she wishes to do?

Look carefully at the implications of decisions you make. Decide on a fair amount of time that you will each take to think about what you've discussed. Come back to the discussion in that agreed amount of time and continue to talk, make your final decision, or take more time for further consideration.

Never drop the ball. It might be tempting to put off some decisions, hoping your daughter will forget about her request. (And by the way, sometimes with the passage of a little time she *will* change her mind.) However, don't try to forget it and dismiss all the time you spent in discussion around it. Don't let the issue drop, just because you think she might forget it. Bring it up at the agreed-upon time and find resolution. If you are struggling with the issue at hand, then you need to explore why. Is it an issue that really needs to be on your "nonnegotiable" list, but you didn't put it there to begin with? Maybe you need more compromise from her before you can be comfortable approving of something. Figure out where you're at, and then be honest with your daughter about it.

Educate your daughter about the issues at hand. What does she need to hear from you before you tackle this issue? Are there safety issues you need to go over with her before coming to any compromise or agreements? If she wants to get a tattoo, you should discuss health risks; if she wants Internet access, you should discuss other safety issues. For example, you would need to educate your daughter about how she could be victimized through conversation, as well as the transfer of sexually explicit information and material, online. Make sure your daughter understands that people who spend large amounts of time online during the evening hours, particularly in chat rooms, are at greater risk of being targeted by computer-sex offenders. It would also be important to talk openly about the natural interest and curiosity adolescents may have about sexuality and sexually explicit material which leads them to actively seek out such materials online. If you decide that monitoring computer use is in your daughter's best interest, explain to her why you may randomly check her e-mail accounts and monitor chat-room activities.

Negotiation is based on trust. Setting limits, enforcing rules, and maintaining active involvement in your daughter's life is important. It does not mean you don't, or can't, trust her. It means you recognize the human factor in all the tough choices and decisions that she's making. It also means you care enough about her that you don't want to thrust temptation directly in her path. For most people, it's too easy to do the wrong thing. For adolescents, the temptation is greater. Regulating and staying involved in what's happening in your daughter's world is not the same as intruding and overprotecting her. Setting good boundaries minimizes the chances that she will make poor choices.

THINK POSITIVE

Someone once said, "What you see is mainly what you look for." Despite the blowups, meltdowns, power struggles, and bickering, expect to be happy with your daughter. What you put into your relationship and what you expect from your relationship are what you are likely to get out of it. Concentrate on cultivating and enjoying a peaceful, happy bond. Spend time with your daughter and maintain a caring touch. These qualities provide a strong foundation for building the kind of positive communication that will inoculate your relationship against the permanently damaging forms of conflict that can so easily tear you apart.

Many mothers that I spoke to had made a commitment to be more open and understanding with their daughters than their own mothers had been with them. Ironically, they believe, it is this very openness that creates conflict in their relationships with their daughters. As one mother explained: "It comes with the territory. If you are going to better inform your daughter about the world, teach her to think for herself, and encourage her self-expression, then expect her to practice it on you. It's the price we pay for a healthier sense of openness, and it's worth it."

STRETCHING EXERCISES

Consider using all or some of the following exercises to help minimize, diffuse, or cope positively with the power struggles you may encounter with your daughter.

Exercise: Look for Positives

When conflict is high and anger abounds, don't get lost in the negative ways you may be feeling toward your daughter. Instead, look for "positives."

★ Make a list of positive behaviors and qualities you notice about your daughter. Actively seek out positive character and personality assets. In what ways is she maturing and growing?

★ Every week, concentrate on at least one of those attributes and compliment her on it. Remember, look for, hope for, and expect the best from her!

Exercise: Mother/Daughter Meetings

Hold weekly meetings for the purpose of sharing important activities, concerns, and projects that you each have going on. Some families of faith choose to use this time to share devotions and prayer time together. The weekly meeting can also be useful for expressing complaints, distributing chores, and setting expectations for the upcoming week, planning mother/daughter fun time, and expressing encouraging and loving things to each other.

★ Establish a regular time and place for your meeting.

★ Agree on a thirty- to forty-five minute time frame and stick to it!

★ Keep a notebook of agenda items you and your daughter wish to address. Add to them during the week as issues come up.

★ Have a "no gripe" rule. Agree to solve problems, not just "gripe." Brainstorm solutions together and encourage creativity in resolving them.

★ Agree to concentrate on listening and communicating.

★ Follow up on agreements made at each meeting.

★ Try starting your meeting off by sharing your "high" points and "low" points of the past week with each other. It's important to share in your daughter's struggles as well as celebrate in her successes and for your daughter to do the same with you. (Note: Weekly meetings are very effective with the entire family as well.)

Exercise: Write a Contract Together

This can be particularly helpful when one or both of you has a problem with the other's behavior and both of you want changes to occur. It's important that you both agree to approach each other with respect and openness.

1. Take ten minutes to make a list of the specific behaviors that you want the other person to change. Identify the three most important to you.

2. Take another ten minutes and list specific behaviors that you want the other person to keep. Choose three things from this list you want to discuss.

3. Discuss with each other the changes you would like to see in the other. Flip a coin to determine who goes first. Read and explain what you have written. You may need to compromise or come up with changes that you both can agree on. Once you do, sign a contract agreeing to these changes.

4. Now share the behaviors you like in the other person from the second list you made and close on a positive note with an agreement to follow up on the contract agreement every week.

Exercise: Write a Letter of Love

Before confronting your daughter about difficult issues or events, try practicing what you have to say on paper. Express yourself by writing from a position of love instead of anger or blame. Explain exactly how you feel, what you feel, and why you feel it. This letter is for your eyes only, but doing this simple exercise can help you go into a discussion feeling centered and clear.

CHAPTER
3

Being the Best Mom
You Can Be

You can guide, lay a foundation of right and wrong, set limits and consequences, but ultimately your daughter will need to make her own decisions and choices. No matter how many books you read, you won't be prepared for it all. And you won't be able to prevent every mistake. Having a teenage daughter puts you on a roller coaster. To be the best mom you can be, just enjoy the ride and love your daughter to pieces.

—Mother of a seventeen-year-old daughter

Your teenage daughter is a work in progress. All the ups and downs of her development play a part in who she is and will become. Roller-coaster rides can be frightening as well as exhilarating, but don't assume that just because you're parenting a teenage daughter you're in for a dangerous ride, or even an unpleasant one. The onslaught of adolescence doesn't mean you are automatically destined for a long, hard struggle.

According to research, less than ten percent of teens have seriously troubled relationships with their families, where there are chronic and escalating levels of conflict and repeated arguments over serious issues (Paikoff and Brooks-Gunn 1991). Not all teens are explosive, out of control, indulging in promiscuous sex, or liars. It's important not to let your fears about adolescence prevent you from seeing your daughter fairly and accurately.

Many mothers experience times of indescribable joy during their daughter's teen years. Others say that even though there *are* struggles and challenges, they aren't overwhelming. Having a clear sense of direction and positive perspective can help.

TOO GOOD TO BE TRUE: THE TEXTBOOK MOM

No matter how many books you read on this subject, you won't be prepared for everything that happens to you as the mother of a teenage daughter. In fact, depending on what you read, you may end up feeling worse after educating yourself. You may believe you will never be able to measure up to, or put into action, the life of a textbook mom. And if so, you're right.

A textbook mom not only lives in books, she lives in magazines, on television, and in the movies. She can be found almost anywhere. And she's perfect. She always looks at least fifteen years younger than she should and never suffers from fatigue, bad hair days, or a stressful professional life. She is always happy and in perfect shape. She loves her family unconditionally seven days a week, has the humility of a saint, the intuition and insight of a genius, and she never loses her temper.

The textbook mom knows all the appropriate developmental tasks that her teenager must accomplish and helps her succeed at each one. As if that weren't enough, her teenager returns her love unconditionally, obeys obligingly, listens openly, respects the wisdom and advice she offers, loves being with her, and never forgets her birthday.

Chances are, if you hold any ideal of a mother that's difficult for you to achieve, you aren't being fair to yourself. Bury the myth. Then, be the best mom you can be, on your own terms.

On Your Own Terms

Begin being the best mom you can be by accepting the fact that you will never be able to love your daughter perfectly all the time.

Many moms have told me they have ended up doing or saying the very things they vowed they would never say or do to their own daughters. Not being able to love your daughter perfectly all the time does not mean you are inept or that you have stopped loving your daughter. Nor is it realistic to expect that you will be able to be rational and practice clear reasoning all the time.

What is realistic and worth aspiring to is living your life in a way that brings you happiness and satisfaction. The mother of two seventeen-year-old-girls wrote:

> When you're happy with yourself and your life, mother-hood is way easier. You can have bad days and blow it sometimes, and have moments of lunacy, but if, at the core of your being, you know you are generally a caring, loving person, your kids don't forget that. I think it's dangerous for girls to think their moms could be faultless. It would be a lie, and a standard they may think they had to meet. In fact, my mistakes show them how to blow it and still be a good person, worthy of forgiveness. Who doesn't need to learn that?

PARENTING PITFALLS

There are a number of negative parenting styles that you should avoid. Beware of any of the pitfalls described below. Don't panic if you see yourself reflected in any of the following descriptions. If one of these negative patterns describes you, however, and you feel stuck and unable to move, seek help and make a commitment to change with the support of a professional counselor or therapist.

Perfectionism breeds discouragement, feelings of inadequacy, self-hatred, and depression because, being great, to a perfectionist, is never great enough. If you are a perfectionist, your daughter will learn to set the same unrealistic standards for herself that you do, creating further despair.

Rejecting behavior is worse than perfectionism because it attacks a girl's spirit, not just her performance. Rejecting your daughter is a hostile, demeaning, and abusive act. Words like, "You're a jerk!" or "You are a pain!" or "I wish you would leave!" are cruel blows. You may reject your daughter more subtly, by not listening or paying attention to her or by putting her off because you'd rather not be bothered. Occasionally, all parents may be subtly rejecting. Your usual response to her is what's most important.

Overprotectiveness can be a problem when mothers have diffi-culty "letting go." If you are always doing for your teen what she is capable of doing for herself, you are communicating to her that you are uncomfortable with her performance and abilities. Many over-protective moms mean well and are very loving, but this behavior fosters dependency and may be a way for you to gain a sense of security and control over your daughter's life. Ultimately, over-protectiveness generates deep feelings of inadequacy and helpless-ness in your daughter. Her personal courage decreases and a sense of strength and independence is thwarted.

Overindulgence is giving too many things to your daughter. Some mothers have a fear of saying "no" and a fear of their daughter's reactions to being denied anything. Some moms are compensating for what they lacked in their own childhood by overindulging their daughters. This practice results in teens not being able to learn the value of working hard to attain a goal or the satisfaction of attaining it. Unable to delay gratification, it may be difficult for your daughter to learn a sense of responsibility and accountability to others.

Overpermissiveness results when there are not enough rules and restrictions on your daughter's behaviors. When there are not enough limits and clearly stated "rights and wrongs," your daughter is likely to have a problem relating to others in healthy ways. She doesn't know the "rules." When her peers demand mutual respect and tolerance, your daughter may react with extreme frustration and a deep sense of alienation. She may not be accustomed to adjusting to others. For this reason, overly permissive moms do an extreme disservice to their daughters.

Severe or *harsh* parenting patterns can be damaging to your daughter and result in deep wounds. There are many forms of severe or harsh behaviors that can be detrimental to your relationship, attack your daughter's self-esteem, and negatively influence her development. If you're worried that your behavior is at times too harsh, you should seek professional help.

Inconsistency is another problem that often results when a mother's own life is out of control. You may be easygoing one day and rigid the next. Your daughter doesn't know what's expected of her. She could develop highly evolved manipulation skills, and lack a strong moral foundation and conscience, because "anything goes."

Guilt-tripping is a subtle and insidious way to keep control over a teenager. It is an opportunity for moms to express their angry dis-appointments and resentments that may or may not have anything to do with their daughters. Girls can't win when their decisions must be made based on pleasing their mothers. In this atmosphere, your daughter is likely to suffer from frustrating self-doubt and distrust of her own self-worth.

Either too much or too little parental involvement in your daughter's life will hamper her growth and maturity. To be the best mom you can be, it's important to find a balance between the right amount of structure and the right amount of freedom. This balance cannot be found at either extreme of permissiveness or rigidity.

MOMS IN THE MIDDLE

According to John DeFrain, the following qualities are found in all healthy families: appreciation and affection, commitment, positive communication, time together, spiritual well-being, and the ability to cope with stress and crisis (Pipher 1994). These important qualities thrive in an atmosphere where teens have enough freedom to grow independently while being nurtured and protected by structure, love, and fair rules. Striking a balance between connection and separation may involve special challenges and adjustments. You will want to establish a special blend of togetherness and independence. When you find that balance, you and your daughter will remain attached and she may continue to seek your advice, but in a context of greater freedom.

Taking an approach that is neither excessively restrictive nor too strict, and is not extremely permissive or totally free of restraints, has been referred to as "democratic" parenting. This middle-of-the-road approach is sensitive to the needs of adolescents and encourages teens to express feelings, make decisions, solve problems, and develop self-esteem and independence. Democratic parenting fosters moral understanding and development in teens, as well. Your daughter can learn the value of parental authority when you set limits, structure her choices, and use discipline that follows natural and logical consequences.

Creating the Right Climate

In this type of atmosphere mothers combine their warmth with high expectations for their daughters. Girls have the advantage of learning to obey out of love rather than fear. If you were to practice this parenting approach, here is how it might look:

* ★ You would encourage your daughter to express opinions and make suggestions freely.

* ★ You and your daughter would regularly practice open discussions, centering on issues related to her behavior, expectations, and decisions.

★ You would routinely explain your rules and expectations.

★ You would be moderately permissive, setting consistent rules within a home that was warm and supportive.

★ You would listen sensitively and ask clarifying questions.

★ You would not lecture, use threats, or make sarcastic remarks.

★ Your teenage daughter would make some of her own decisions, but you would always have the final authority in all decision-making.

★ You would moderate your sense of protectiveness by allowing your daughter to take appropriate risks.

★ You would minimize dominance and control, and you and your daughter's appreciation for one another would be high.

★ The two of you would openly express affection, communicate positively, and negotiate frequently.

★ You and your daughter would balance time together with time apart.

★ The emphasis would be on learning from each other, working together, and valuing each other as individuals of equal worth.

★ You would listen to and respect your daughter's interests, needs, thoughts, and feelings.

★ You, your daughter, and other family members would share a steady and solid bond.

★ In your home, harmony, good humor, tolerance, and understanding would be in ample supply.

Does a home like this sound too good to be true? Keep in mind that you could never live up to all these qualities all the time. It's simply not possible. However, by setting high standards for your parenting style and approach, you can guide your family in positive directions that will only lead to greater harmony.

Coping with Stress and Worry

Most mothers try to do their best in raising daughters. But, as discussed earlier, every mom has her limitations, particularly when she's under stress. Excess worry may cause you to react in ways that are damaging to your relationship with your daughter. As a way to lessen her anxiety, one mother I interviewed found it helpful to continually remind herself of the following: "No matter what's happening, I just take a deep breath and know what's going to happen is going to happen. We can't control everything. You have to trust yourself. You know your daughter better than anyone."

It's not easy being a mother, and most parents find themselves in the job without many skills. Most parents are not prepared for the demands of raising children and, at times, may find it too difficult to handle. If any of the following stress factors are present in your life, it's important to seek professional help; frustration and stress can quickly lead to child abuse. Seek help if you:

★ were abused as a child

★ feel isolated

★ have a poor self-image

★ hold unrealistic expectations or standards for your daughter

★ experience depression because you are disappointed in your teen's behavior

★ abuse alcohol or drugs

★ are afraid to discipline your daughter for fear of losing control

★ have an unsympathetic or abusive mate

If any of these or other demands on you become too great, it's important to be willing to reach out into the community for assistance. Don't delay. Contact a parent support organization or women's center as soon as possible.

Also remember that the difficulties your daughter may encounter are not necessarily your fault. Your teenager is a complex person influenced by physiological predispositions, peers, school, and the culture as a whole. Some difficulties simply stem from the challenges inherent in being a teenager.

HORMONES AND HEAT WAVES: MOTHERS IN MENOPAUSE

Unfortunately, many mothers are going through their own major period of developmental adjustment just as their daughters are going through adolescence. It's not unusual to be in some phase of menopause during your daughter's teen years. Perimenopause, full-blown, or postmenopause is a reminder that your fertility has ended or is coming to an end and that the part of you that gave your daughter life is no longer viable.

One mother came to the realization this way:

> I said, "No way am I having a hysterectomy! Why would I do that when I still want another baby?" Even though I would not even try it at forty-five, the longing was oddly real. Then when I had suffered through enough prolonged bleeding, even to the point of hemorrhaging, I suddenly woke up one morning and said to myself, "Why in the world am I trying so hard to save something that's trying to kill me?" I packed my bags and went into surgery the next day. It was a huge relief, no longer a loss. I had to go through this strange process of mourning. Now I realize my daughter will always be living proof of my once healthy uterus! And I've found new freedom in the deal.

There are new freedoms in this passage, but to get there women have to navigate their way through the changing tides of hormones. Another mom told me this:

> No one told me the real reason raising teens is so hard. It's because most of us are tackling menopause at the same time that our daughters are raging in PMS. It's too much. Between my full-time job, being a mother of a teen, hot flashes, and trying to plan for retirement, I resent having to look at hormonal choices and changes on top of everything else. Besides, I don't like seeing the proof of my age. I wanted to always remain a young mother.

During this stage in your own development, you may be reassessing your own life and finding that the possibilities are narrowing. One forty-eight-year-old mother explained her experience this way:

> I just realized that, once my daughter became a teenager, my life as I knew it, and had become so accustomed to, would soon be over. I mean, motherhood will soon be over for me. I know they say motherhood is never over, but let's face it, she'll go off to college and get married, and my job will be done. Then what? This is the job I know best! Now I find that I'm desperate to do things with my daughter and try to be with her as much as possible while I still can, and it drives her crazy. She's ready to fly, and I just figured out she's going to have to leave me. It sounds ridiculous, but it just never hit me this way until now.

Expanding Your Horizons

If you're between the ages of forty and fifty, you may be using a significant amount of emotional energy coping with your own changes in midlife. What most mothers show us, however, is that they can continue to grow and expand their personal horizons. A forty-nine-year-old mother told me:

> Now that my daughter is seventeen, it's time for me to get back to doing something for myself. I have been volunteering in the schools for years and it's been great, but I don't want to find myself in the empty-nest syndrome, with nothing left to do but feel sad. I'm planning now to actively seek out work that I really want to do. And you know, I'm kind of excited. I'm looking forward to the personal satisfaction of doing something I feel good at and can be successful in again.

It's not uncommon for mothers to say that their teenage daughters are an inspiration to them. The mother of three teenage daughters said this:

> When my girls became teens, I had to reinvent myself. Because they were older and coming into their own, I had to learn how to be a friend and mother to them. Then, the more they began to grow away from me, the more I rediscovered the parts of myself that I chose to put on hold for a while. For me, that was my creativity. I love to write and paint. I recently wrote and illustrated my own book. It was so much fun. My girls were blown away! I'm not sure they knew what to think about it at first; they just seemed sort of amazed. I just never had the time to really take on these projects before. Now I have the freedom to indulge in my art. I also painted all the walls in our home new colors and themes. My girls say they think it's great and seem a little astonished at how much I love this part of my life. They're an inspiration to me, too. I watch them with so much admiration and respect as they each pursue their dreams and ambitions and talents. They are all so different, with so many gifts. I want them to see that life can be dynamic at any age. I look forward to the new lives we all have ahead of us.

By attending to their daughters during the teen years, mothers often find that a new and satisfying period of life awaits them. The future relationship you have to look forward to with your *adult* daughter also lies ahead. Change can continue to be exciting and satisfying no matter what your age.

SHARING YOUR WISDOM AND ADVICE

Mothers who get together and share their failures and successes can be a tremendous support to one another. It can help to talk to other mothers about your fears, doubts, and greatest concerns. Sharing advice and ideas from your own experiences can be invaluable.

Straight Talk from Moms

★ *Enjoy all the silliness. My husband gets irritated with four teenage girls in the house and he'll say, "Why do they have to be so silly?" and I say, "Aren't they cute?"*

★ *Enjoy her developing personality. Embrace the experience and step back when you need to. They're mature one minute and regressed the next. Don't take anything too seriously or too personally.*

★ *I try and think back to what did or didn't work with my mother, what I liked and didn't like about the way I was raised, and then I try and do it differently for my daughter. I think we should always improve from generation to generation. I hope my daughter will improve on me.*

★ *Every girl is different. You have to find your own way to your daughter. Books can help with ideas, but it's really your own personal job to figure out the best way to connect with your own daughter. She's unique and unlike anyone else you'll ever know.*

★ *Get involved in her life and stay involved. Try not to be intrusive, but be there!*

★ *I want to maintain the traditional values I grew up with, but I want to tweak them a little. I find that keeping the traditional family structure of family meals and activities is important, but then I've updated it with more openness, discussion, and direct communication.*

★ *We're different mothers today. We've progressed. I like adapting a new openness with what I grew up with. It's the best of both worlds for us.*

★ *I make a point of telling my daughter's friends what I respect and admire about their moms. I think we need to do this for each other. Sometimes it's easier to help girls see the positive when they hear it from others. It can give them a feeling of pride, too.*

★ *When I can relax and just enjoy being a mom, the problems we face don't seem quite so insurmountable. I've given up trying to be a supermom because, quite frankly, I'm not a supermom and never will be. But I love my daughter and I enjoy her, and she knows it. I've concluded that that's all that really matters.*

WANTED: LOVING MOM

When I sat down with groups of teenage girls, they discussed what they would want to put in a classified ad if they were going to try and recruit a "great mom" for someone who didn't have one.

Here's what they wrote:

WANTED: Loving mom. Perfect women need not apply. Ideal candidate will be affectionate, available, encouraging, fair, faithful, flexible, forgiving, generous, honest, non-defensive, optimistic, responsible, spontaneous, stable, tolerant, dependable, and someone a daughter can look up to. Must be willing to admit her mistakes. Must have high self-esteem, a great sense of humor, and enjoy her job if she works outside the home. Must have outstanding communication skills with teens. The successful candidate will know what kinds of questions to ask, will not interrupt, will talk nicely, and know how to really listen. Daughter will be able to hear opinions, not commands from woman hired. Must be open to buying groceries requested by daughter sometimes. Must not force her to eat things that make her want to totally puke! Organization is a plus! Must be able to juggle multiple tasks. Must be willing to do a lot with daughter and eat dinner together. Winning candidate for this job will be someone who is supportive, full of laughter, joy, and who isn't "fake." This mom will be HAPPY. And she will have a positive attitude. Must be able to respect privacy and space when needed. Must agree not to worry too much. Must trust daughter. Person selected will agree to leave some of the decisions about her daughter's dates, friends, looks, clothes, hair, and privileges up to her. (Note: Experience preferred but not required for right person. No pay. Great future! Benefits include a happy and cool teenage daughter to go shopping with.)

NOTHING LASTS FOR LONG

It's perhaps trite to say "this too shall pass," but someday you will be looking back on your daughter's adolescence with recollections of how it went. Women who feel they truly did the best they could look back with less regret and greater appreciation. Many grow sentimental and long to have those years back with their daughters. As one mother told me: "It requires so much patience to be a good mother. Seriously, I think patience will make you the best mom you can be. It will all be over so soon. Sooner than you want most times. Be patient through the difficult times. You'll be missing her soon enough."

Make Room for Mistakes and Growth

Part II of this book will address the many challenges your daughter is likely to face during her teen years. Being prepared for the often complex and varied concerns you must personally deal with as a mother during your daughter's adolescence will help you move through it with greater ease. Once you have accepted your limitations, pledge to be the best mom you can be, and remember to allow yourself what you need to allow your daughter—room for mistakes and room to grow in.

STRETCHING EXERCISES

Use the following exercises to help you become the best mom you can be.

Exercise: The Mom Test

How would your daughter rate you as a mom? Read each of the following statements and check the response *you think* your daughter would make. Then read them to your daughter and mark her answers next to yours, or let her complete the test and compare responses. Use a scale of 1–4, where 1 is "never," 2 is "sometimes," 3 is "usually," and 4 is "always."

_____ I can rely on my mom to help me, even when I'm not able to ask for the help I want.

_____ My mom has time for me.

_____ My mom is emotionally supportive.

_____ When my mom disagrees with me, she is not angry, judging, or critical.

_____ I value my mom's opinions.

_____ My mom does whatever is within her power to create a peaceful and harmonious atmosphere in our home.

_____ I totally trust my mom.

_____ My mom has my welfare and best interests in mind when she is making decisions about me.

_____ My mom seeks my opinions, ideas, and input into her decision-making process.

_____ My mom really listens to me.

_____ My mom can understand my feelings from my point of view.

_____ I can describe what my mom's beliefs and values are.

_____ My mom finds humor in life.

_____ My mom and I laugh together.

_____ My mom and I have fun together.

_____ I am proud of my mom.

Discuss the results with your daughter. How do her responses compare to what you expected her to say? Were there any that surprised you? What responses did your daughter expect from you? Were there any that surprised her? What would you both like to change? Make a plan to practice some new ways of relating if necessary.

Exercise: Creating Harmony

1. Sit down with your daughter and silently write your own definitions for "harmony."

2. Share your responses.

3. Write a sentence telling how you can build or improve harmony in your relationship.

4. Exchange your statements and come up with a way to act on the ideas you each wrote down.

5. Post them somewhere and follow up on how you're doing every week.

Exercise: Give Yourself a Reality Check

Find someone who can give you a reality check when you need or want one. Meet with a mothers' support group, friends, your husband or partner, or a counselor on a regular basis to talk about your struggles and successes as a mom. It's helpful to bounce things off someone and hear from others how they think you're doing. It's also a great way to learn new ideas and approaches that work for others.

PART
II

Empowering Your Daughter

CHAPTER 4

Through a Storm of Emotions

I'm sitting in my room right now in tears. I hate my life! It totally sucks. I've been crying and mad all day. I don't know why! I think I'm depressed. I wish I could tell someone, but I can't. I don't want anyone to know that I have serious problems. Oh yeah, our team is going to play in the finals tomorrow and everyone thinks we will win. I hope so! I am sooooooo bored right now. Nobody is home or online, and my mom won't let me take calls anyway because I've been yelling at her all day. I am in such a crappy mood. I hate it. Except for this! I almost forgot! Today before third period Miguel gave me his school picture!! He signed the back and said "Love Ya!" I am so excited! He is so sweet and hot! I love him so much! Now I have to go do chores, which is so lame to make me do. Like I don't have anything better to do with my life than bury dog poop. LOL! TTYL!

—Diary entry from a fourteen-year-old girl

When a school counselor read the above entry, she nodded her head and said, "Just another typical day in the life of a teenage girl." In the time it took this girl to make just one entry in her diary she had expressed sadness, anger, loneliness, depression, excitement, boredom, frustration, love, and humor. It may be exhausting for you to think about, let alone experience with your own daughter, but if your daughter is like most teens, she rarely seems to tire from chasing an endless train of emotions.

The moods and passions percolating in your daughter can plummet up and down as dramatically as an airplane hitting a wind shear. Some days are likely to be more volatile than others, but for most teens, feelings are in a constant state of motion. It's common for her to go through one or more cycles of mood swings each day. Consequently, your daughter's emotional forecast may be difficult to predict. In order to help your daughter weather the emotional storms that may loom on the horizon, you can offer her shelter, prepare her for the elements, and teach her how to survive them. She will need the freedom to feel, a way to safely express herself, and the time to practice coping skills for the full range of her emotions.

BLAME IT ON HORMONES, NEURO-TRANSMITTERS, AND FULL MOONS

Moms often ask what catapults their daughters into such extreme states of emotional distress and energy. After her daughter threw her arms around her in a warm embrace one moment and then slammed a door in her face the next, one perplexed mother asked, "What is *that*?"

You can always blame it on hormones. Premenstrual syndrome (PMS) is alive and well in most young girls who have hit puberty, as are mood swings related to fluctuating hormones. Girls and their mothers often see emotional changes occurring in the week before their periods. Moods may be positive at mid-cycle, and sadness and anger are most often seen in the days prior to periods starting. But recent research has also acknowledged the role of the still developing adolescent brain, especially in the areas related to impulse control and extreme shifts in emotions.

Because the brain is not yet fully mature (or as someone told me, "My teens don't seem to be operating with a full deck yet"), adolescents may naturally have less control over some of their emotions and reactions. Many women collectively breathe a sigh of relief as their daughters grow older. Most say they grow to be reasonable and easy again once they hit their later teen years and become physically more mature.

But while they're young, their behavior baffles those closest to them. The mother of a fifteen year-old-daughter described a scene that took place in her home one evening:

It was my daughter's day to do the dishes and because she put the task off for so long she ended up with twice as much to do. When she finally stomped into the kitchen to fulfill her responsibility, the cupboard doors and drawers started flinging open and shut with careless abandon. I had something I wanted to tell her and decided to go ahead and share my news even if she wasn't in the best of moods.

"*I Love Lucy* went to Paris in last night's episode," I reported. "I've seen it," she replied dryly, still banging dishes around. "The one where she goes alone to an outdoor café to eat lunch?" I asked. "Oh," she said thoughtfully, "I'm not sure I saw that one." And then in full force she announced, "You know, maybe everyone should try loading their own dirty, disgusting dishes into the dishwasher, so I don't get stuck having to do this whole disgusting load by myself!" "It might work in the future," I acknowledged. "Some of these supposedly *clean* dishes are *dirty*, Mom!" "You did the last load, not me," I reminded her. "I know how to do the dishes. I'm not that stupid! Obviously you think I am!" Her voice cracked and her eyes dampened.

"Okay," she continued, "why is this gross and disgusting meat fat still lying on the counter? Hel-lo! Why haven't you thrown it in the trash?" "As tonight's clean-up crew, do whatever you need to do," I said graciously. Then I asked her, "Do you remember the part where Lucy plugs her nose with the escargot tongs?" My daughter cracked up laughing. I explained the show in more detail. But then her voice boomed again when she suddenly bellowed out, "You know, people need to throw away their own dirty, gross napkins so I don't have to touch them all!" "I know the feeling," I told her. I continued, "Then Lucy gets arrested for passing counterfeit money." "Yeah! I did see that part!" she said excitedly.

The dishwasher slammed shut so quickly I asked if she had put the soap in. "Yes I put the soap in!" she screamed. "Don't you *trust* me? Check up on me, why don't ya!" She flipped the start switch and stomped out of the kitchen in a bucket of tears. My husband and I locked eyes. "She's got PMS big-time," I started to explain. "It is a hormonal problem." "It sounds like a problem all right," he confirmed. I added, "You know, they say because their brain development isn't complete, they have trouble with impulse control at this age, too. Maybe she's not all connected yet.

Maybe her synapses are misfiring, or her neurotransmitters aren't plugged in, do you think?" "Something," he replied. I continued, "You know it's a full moon tonight, too. That throws everyone out of whack." He looked at me skeptically, just as my daughter graced us with her presence again. This time she made a grand entrance, marching to the drums banging in the movie we were attempting to watch. She paraded around the room, laughing hysterically at herself. We laughed, too. She had obviously flipped a switch in her head, right after the one on the dishwasher.

It's normal to want reasons for illogical, confusing behaviors. As the mother of a teenager, you will find yourself often searching for answers. Sometimes it's easier to accept the fact that any number of factors may be influencing your daughter. A good deal of the time, physiological states will be the culprit, but situational factors influence moodiness, too. Negative life events, problems in school, with boys, and with friends can also make feelings less stable. And some people blame it on the full moon.

Fasten Your Seat Belt

What seems certain is that an emotional roller coaster is bound to take off during these years, and you will need to deal with it the best and most creative ways you know how. The mother of a sixteen-year-old girl said, "I can rest easier when I remember how crazy I felt as a teenager. I even scared myself sometimes, I would feel so emotional and out of control. I think it's important to share our own experiences with our daughters, so they know they aren't unusual."

There are some key points to keep in mind as you prepare to help your daughter understand the strong emotional reactions that seem to control her at times.

What You Can Do

★ Tell her that emotions themselves are neither good nor bad. It's what she learns to do with her feelings and how she responds to them that can be judged positively or negatively.

★ Help your daughter learn how to express herself without using emotions to manipulate situations or people. It's common for teens to try and use their emotions to get what they want. Encouraging her to express feelings honestly and openly will help.

★ Remember, emotional reactions, even in extreme forms, are appropriate at your daughter's age. Understanding this can help you feel less confused when she seems to overreact to seemingly minor issues.

Helping your daughter come to terms with her emotions in a healthy way will provide her with a valuable lesson. You both may feel like you're trying to tame a bucking bronco at times, but don't give up. She needs your help in understanding her feelings and she especially needs your help in learning how to accept and manage the sometimes wild and unyielding beast of emotions that can engulf her.

STORM WARNINGS

When high winds blow into town, the local forecaster instructs people to "tie down what you can and secure yourself." This may also be good advice for mothers of teenage girls. The mother of a fifteen-year-old girl said this: "We have a 'Hurricane Hannah' living in our home. When she starts gaining emotional momentum, everyone knows it and that's our signal to prepare ourselves. We say to each other, 'Hurricane Hannah is home. Batten down the hatches.' Then we brace ourselves."

More often than not, mothers say they can usually read the changes in their daughter's moods and attitudes. They know something's "off" and that she's troubled, but it's hard for most moms to know what to do next. As one mom put it: "Every situation is so different. I spend so much time trying to figure out what to do, I do nothing! More often than not, I feel like a bulldozer just ran over me and then I'm completely immobilized."

Shelter from the Storm

Loving moms often try to come up with something tangible they can do to help their daughters feel better. Rather than expend the energy on trying to solve your daughter's problems, consider offering her the protective space in which to express her feelings. This is the first step to helping your daughter learn from her emotions. Here's an example of how one mother has helped her sixteen-year-old daughter feel safe expressing her feelings to her:

When my daughter has an emotional meltdown, she usually directs it at me, so I immediately try to do some quick damage control. I put whatever I'm doing aside and calmly sit and listen to her complete outburst. Feelings spew everywhere, but I can usually follow what she's saying. Sometimes I'll ask her to clarify something, but I'll keep it simple. Anyway, she spews, I listen, she cries, I empathize, she runs to her room, and I take a deep breath and carry on with what I was doing. Later, we'll talk about what happened and what her choices were for the way she was feeling. It looks like high drama to everyone else, but to my daughter it's very real and very important. I try not to discount any of my daughter's feelings and I try to help her get a handle on them at the same time. Over time, I've seen a dramatic improvement in her ability to reason through and cope with tough feelings. She can even admit now when she's been unbearable. We talk about it, as a matter of fact. I have always assured her, it would get better as she matured, and sure enough, it has.

The capacity to show positive feelings grows when teens find love, affection, companionship, acceptance, respect, and approval from those around them. Girls who are happy, optimistic, warm, and affectionate often live in secure environments filled with pleasurable activities and close interpersonal relationships. It's been said that "how you feel is how you act." If your home is filled with more strife than harmony, you are likely to experience more extreme forms of acting out from your teen.

To better prepare for your daughter's most challenging moments, it will help if you become familiar with some of the most common emotions that cause both mothers and daughters the greatest grief.

ANGER

Anger is an energy-charged emotion. It may be one of the most uncomfortable and scary feelings to deal with. But unless anger becomes destructively intense, it is a completely normal and healthy feeling, and your daughter will have it.

Anger may take the form of verbal aggression and may include swearing, arguing, shouting, or dissolving into temper tantrums. Swearing can be used to show defiance, but it also reinforces feelings of autonomy. Your teenager may use language you don't approve of to help demonstrate the generation gap that exists between you.

Some girls tend to hold in their feelings of anger and sulk, withdraw, or become moody instead. When excessive and uncontrollable anger builds up and is not expressed in constructive ways, it can take impulsive, irrational, and destructive forms.

It's important to help your daughter understand the difference between healthy self-expression and abusive forms of anger. Modeling healthy forms is the best way to teach your daughter to express the same. Setting clear and appropriate limits will also help you provide her with ways to put some structure and safety around strong emotions.

Getting to the Root of It

You may experience your daughter's anger more often before her period starts, but there are other provocations. Possible causes include:

✶ the need to push away from parents or other authority figures

✶ the desire to regain a sense of control over her life

✶ the need to express feelings of hurt disguised by anger

✶ experiencing attacks on her ego

✶ feeling criticized

✶ being denied the opportunity for a social life

✶ being shamed

✶ being belittled

✶ experiencing rejection

✶ feeling incompetent and "stupid"

✶ feeling discouraged and apathetic

Be tolerant of your daughter's self-expression when she is directing hostile energy into creative and constructive outlets. Acknowledge the times she successfully redirects her anger or expresses it to others in a clear and nondefensive manner. Most teenage daughters need help learning how to live with anger. They need consistent, positive role models to show them how anger can be turned into a benefit rather than a detriment.

Mothers and daughters shared what they do when anger strikes.

Straight Talk from Daughters

✶ *I go into my room, sometimes I slam my door just because it feels good. Then I listen to my music or read to take my mind off my feelings for a while. I need to be alone.*

★ *I used to cry and stomp down the hallway and sometimes I still do cry because I'm very emotional. My mom is very emotional, too. It's unusual for us not to cry in the movies. I like to watch them, so I can cry and that helps me get it out and feel better.*

★ *I cuss and swear. Usually at myself, but sometimes I direct it at my mom. I try to write it in my journal instead of taking it out on her, but she swears at me too, and then there's no stopping me.*

★ *I hide out in my room. I listen to music and cut out my favorite pictures from magazines.*

★ *And sometimes it's really annoying when you're trying to be alone and someone comes and tells you that you have to go do something. I just want to throw something at them!*

★ *I pour out my anger on the pages of my diary.*

Straight Talk from Moms

★ *Let her talk about it. She needs to vent and be heard.*

★ *I try my best not to give her back the same outburst of anger in return.*

★ *I encourage my daughter to communicate her anger to the person she is angry with.*

★ *I tell my daughter to pull out of the situation. I tell her to take some space, get some distance from what's setting her off, and take a time-out to think it through. I want to help her slow down her response.*

★ *I point out what's good about anger. Sometimes it corrects an unfair situation or can even protect you from harm. When I'm angry or getting angry, that's the first thing I say. Then I explain why. That's how I want my daughter to deal with it, so I try to set the example.*

★ *I put on music, encourage her to take a walk with me, soak in a hot bath, and go for a run with her dog, or whatever she can do to release her anger in a helpful way.*

★ *A counselor told me there's always hurt under anger, so I ask her what she might feel hurt about. Once we approach her anger from that standpoint, everything changes. She softens and we can really talk about what the problem was.*

★ *I leave her alone because that's what she tells me she needs. But I always let her know I'm willing to talk when she's ready, and that I expect her to talk at some point.*

★ *I offer her forgiveness when her anger's been directed at me and when it's time to let it go.*

SADNESS

Teenagers often experience sadness. Your daughter may feel sad at fairly frequent intervals, and it does not necessarily mean that she is seriously or clinically depressed. Sadness is mild depression and results in a temporary loss of energy, a need to be alone, irritability, tearfulness, or withdrawal.

Adolescent girls will experience sadness in response to a variety of different situations or experiences. For most teens, it's helpful and necessary for them to spend some time alone in order to refuel and replenish their emotional health and energy. Mothers and daughters shared other strategies for coping with sadness.

Straight Talk from Daughters

★ *I go into my room and do something distracting. I read a book, play on my computer, or, if I'm really upset, sometimes I'll write in my diary about why I'm sad, and that'll make me happy again. It helps to let it out.*

★ *I can't read when I'm upset. I can't understand or concentrate on what I'm looking at when I'm sad. It doesn't work. I put my music on and write in my journal or write a letter to my best friend.*

★ *I'm more emotional now than when I was little. When my feelings are hurt, I start crying and I don't quit until I've gotten it all out.*

★ *I always think about children in other places who have so much more to be sad about than me.*

Straight Talk from Moms

★ *I tell her that I notice she seems sad, and then I ask what I can do to help. I never try to talk her out of her moods because that makes it worse for my daughter.*

★ *It helps to comfort her with affection if she wants it. Otherwise I may bring her a hot cup of cocoa, some flowers for her room, or suggest we play some cards or another game.*

★ *I tell her it's okay to cry and feel grief. Even when there hasn't been a death, we talk about what loss she's feeling from whatever situation's made her feel bad. I think it's important to help our girls learn how to identify the source of their feelings. I think it helps them to move through sadness easier when they do.*

★ *My daughter goes through this whole pain and suffering thing when really she's just bored. She can become so sad and dramatic that you think she's lost her best friend. I encourage her to use her creativity and take responsibility for herself. I tell her how confident I am that she will be able to figure out something interesting to do. If that doesn't work, I assign a few extra chores. It's amazing how resourceful she suddenly becomes!*

FEAR AND ANXIETY

Fear and anxiety are common emotional experiences for most teenage girls. Some girls are less prone to anxiety than others. Heredity and environmental factors influence a predisposition to worry. Uncontrollable life events can also stimulate anxiety and fear in teenage girls. Excessive amounts of fear and anxiety may make girls more prone to depression.

New challenges, experiences, and changes are plentiful in adolescence and require ongoing adjustments. Fears can carry over from childhood. Common fears for girls include a fear of things (real or imagined), fear for self and others (safety concerns), fear in social relationships, and fear of the unknown.

Lack of self-confidence will exacerbate anxiety, so it is important to give your daughter a great deal of encouragement. Help her find opportunities to achieve some significant successes.

Straight Talk from Daughters

★ *When I'm nervous about doing something, I get grumpy and mad. Then if my mom figures out why, she talks to me about it and we come up with a way for me to do what I have to do, but with some ideas to make it a little easier.*

★ *I try and remember that everyone gets afraid and nervous sometimes. It helps me to talk to my friends about it.*

★ *I don't like to be alone when I'm afraid. As soon as I have something fun to do or have a friend over, it helps me to forget about whatever I was afraid of.*

★ *I hate to fly. I try and relax, but it's really, really hard. I'm so afraid of the plane crashing. My mom talks me through it by explaining all the noises, and reminds me of how many planes fly every day without crashing. She shows me how to take slow, deep breaths and relax my muscles. Then she reminds me that there are things in life that are out of our control and we have to trust in our faith. Then when we land, I'm like, hey, that was fun! Let's go again!*

Straight Talk from Moms

★ *My daughter gets stomachaches when she's afraid and anxious. I try and help her recognize what her fears are about, so she can get some control over them. I teach her to take deep breaths and then talk about the worst thing that could happen in the situation she is worried about. Then we talk about how she would deal with every scenario she comes up with. She needs to find ways she can have control over her anxiety, so the fears don't control her.*

★ *Because of what we believe, I've taught my daughter to use prayer. I tell her, "Go to God when you're upset about something. Ask for help. Talk. Use spiritual resources."*

★ *I understand my daughter's anxiety because I've suffered from it my whole life. One night, one of her best friends was celebrating her birthday with a dance party. She dreaded going because, as much as she loved her friend, some of the people invited were often rude and unfriendly to her. She was dreading being left out and not having anyone to talk to or dance with. I told her I was confident she could handle anything that happened. Then, I reminded her that she didn't have to be comfortable going, but she could go anyway. I told her, "You have every right to have as much fun at this party as anyone else. Walk in there and be friendly and happy and act like you're having a great time even if you aren't. Just fake it! If you're nervous, pretend you're not. If you're lonely, behave as if you weren't." She courageously went in. She had fun and coped well with the awkward moments. The best part is she's glad she went and didn't back out. It was a learning experience.*

STRESS

Your daughter's emotions can affect her physical well-being and health. Just because your daughter is young doesn't mean she won't struggle with real pressures, and her entire body participates in and reacts to an emotional experience, especially under stress. Hectic schedules, activities, homework, deadlines, exams, relationships with friends and boys, chores, her emerging sexuality, and growing sense of independence can all result in strong emotional reactions.

Girls who are discouraged and less optimistic and hopeful are more likely to show signs of stress. Anger, irritability, social withdrawal, nervousness, upset stomach, sleeping problems, eating problems, high blood pressure, headaches, skin problems, and other physical symptoms can all be induced by stress. Some stress is inevitable. Too much, however, can be a burden girls are not designed to carry.

Straight Talk from Daughters

★ *I have to do something physical. I usually go for a run or shoot hoops. That helps me get it out.*

★ *I start eating sweets under stress. Cookies!*

★ *When I'm upset, I call up one of my friends, and it helps me feel better instantly. It's uplifting, and I get someone else's advice.*

★ *I sit alone and pray.*

★ *I spill my guts out to my journal. It helps me to relax when I write.*

Straight Talk from Moms

★ *Academic stress is hardest for my girls. They have constant projects and deadlines. It's always something. What seems to get them through it best of all is giving them a lot of empathy. I tell them, "I know what you're going through. This is really frustrating. I'm amazed you have yet another thing due." I teach them to take it a step at a time. And then I make sure I always point out the light at the end of the tunnel. I remind them, "Saturday, you get a break! This experience is not forever."*

★ *I don't know that I give my daughter much help with stress. I don't think I've been able to teach her, because that's an issue for me. The one thing I have learned to do is turn off the television and put on music to help calm her down.*

★ *I encourage her to take breaks from whatever's stressing her out and give her permission not to be perfect. I tell her, sometimes it's okay to do the best you can and then let it go.*

★ *Come back to it later if it's important.*

★ *My daughter would rather lie on the sofa and do nothing. It's not unusual for her to be up every night at ten o'clock crying, "I can't do this!" and she hasn't even tried. I teach her how to break it down, not to panic, and to get help from teachers when she needs it. Then I remind her when Friday comes she can lie on the sofa and do nothing!*

★ *My daughter has more stress socially. I've found that through our church community there are other adults who love, support, and build her up, and it's a great stress reducer.*

LOVE

Don't underestimate your daughter's ability and capacity to experience genuine love. It is a sign of increasing emotional maturity. Even though mothers don't generally take "young love" and "budding romance" seriously, teenage girls do. They are often sincere about the depths of their emotional experience and find great meaning in their lives from being "in love."

The power of love can encourage positive responses from adults and teens alike. It is the driving force in all intimate relationships, friendships, and in your daughter's relationship with you. Your daughter's emotional experience of love could help her curb aggressive behaviors, heal hurts, and renew her sense of hope and vitality.

Developing loving relationships is one important way your daughter can begin to reach out beyond herself. Loving relationships not only involve the opposite sex but include intense "best friend" relationships, too. Any loving friendship provides your daughter with a rich opportunity to further her emotional maturity. It is appropriate at this age for her time and energy to be spent with peers. Teenage girls want and need to learn about the power and strength of love.

Straight Talk from Daughters

★ *I don't want my mom asking me about "who I like" all the time. She makes too big a deal about it when she knows and acts like I'm going to marry him or something. It's way embarrassing. It helps when she stays out of it.*

★ *My mom's cool. I can tell her everything. It's my dad who freaks out on me. My mom gives me good advice about crushes and how to handle them. She's been through it all.*

★ *Sometimes I come home in a really bad mood because the guy I like dumped me or something. I tell a friend and write in my diary, but my mom doesn't understand.*

★ *My mom lectures me all the time about not letting myself get too serious, and that it's only puppy love and I need to keep my feet on the ground. Ha! If she only knew!*

★ *My friends pretty much know everything, and I go to them when I'm bummed out about a relationship.*

★ *Right now my best friend is the only one who completely understands me, knows me, and loves me anyway! We can go to each other about everything. And we do.*

★ *I read a lot of magazines about love and relationships.*

★ *My mom tells me stories about things that happened to her. It's kind of hard to imagine my mom falling in love because she's been with my dad so long, but it's kind of cool to hear she was a teenager once.*

Straight Talk from Moms

★ *It's hard for my daughter to talk to me about boys. I think she wants me to think she "knows it all" already. Once in a while she'll tell me something, but if I ask too many questions, she clams right up and I never hear another thing. It helps when I don't sound too interested or overreact like I usually do.*

★ *My daughter's so happy when she's with either one of her two best friends. They absolutely love each other. I think it's great. I met my first "soul mate" when I was just thirteen. To this day, we are still the best of friends, proving that you are mature enough to develop serious relationships even at thirteen! It's so important to have a soul mate at this age. It's incredibly helpful.*

★ *I do what I can to help my daughter spend time with special friends who so clearly enrich her life.*

★ *I encourage my daughter to form both male and female friendships. I talk to my daughter about the importance of being able to like a boy, not just as a crush, but also as a good friend.*

Love or Infatuation?

It may be important to help your daughter distinguish between love and infatuation as she travels down the road to romance. But many girls don't want lectures and resent being told how and when they should experience love. It helps to wait for the right time, but when the opportunity arises, you can begin by sharing what you know to be true about love and relationships. Start by teaching your daughter the difference between love, infatuation, and obsessions. Give her examples from your own experiences when you can.

What You Can Say

★ "Mature love is based on real knowledge of the other person. There is a sense of fulfillment and happiness that grows slowly and is lasting."

★ "Love involves your whole personality, not just parts. It includes friendship, admiration, care, and concern, as well as a possible sexual attraction."

★ "Infatuation happens toward someone you may not even know."

★ "Infatuation and obsessions with people often cause frustration, anguish, insecurity, and disappointment."

★ "Infatuation arises quickly and can fade quickly."'

★ "Infatuation can center on intense emotion and strong sexual feelings."

The mother of a family of five teenagers offered this advice:

I tell all my kids, "Don't give away your heart too soon." I am always encouraging them to go slow and wait. I tell them, "The parts of your heart you give away, you don't get back. Save your heart for the real thing. You'll never regret it once you find a real and lasting love. You'll be glad you saved your whole heart for him or her."

HOW TO MEND A BROKEN HEART

There may come a day when you wish you had the ability to go in and fix your daughter's broken heart and replace her pain with new and positive emotions. It's normal for most mothers to agonize along with their daughters when they are suffering emotionally. Experiencing some agony on your daughter's behalf is to be expected, but if it prevents you from being able to be there for her, your own agony will probably only compound her distress.

The mother of a thirteen-year-old girl shared this experience:

My daughter moved to a new school and didn't have any friends when she first started. Late one night, all these feelings just poured out of her. She began sobbing so hard she couldn't talk. She finally said, "I have no friends, I'm ugly, I'm not popular, I'm not hip. Nobody likes me!" As a mom, you just don't want your child to ever have to experience that kind of emotional pain, because it's so awful and cruel. My heart just sank. I could've burst into tears.

A part of me was grasping for a way to hurry and make it all better. I thought to myself, "Okay, I'll take her shopping tomorrow! I'll let her streak her hair and pierce her navel! Whatever she wants, we'll do it so she can be happy again!" Of course that's not what I really said. I wanted to go punish all those kids for being so mean to my "little girl." I wanted to protect her. I felt like a mama bear or lioness. So I had all these feelings and I thought to myself, "Hold on. I need to be the mother." So I started by saying to her, "This is hard. It's so hard to be your age. I felt like this at your age, too. And you may not believe this, but almost every girl in your class probably feels exactly the way you do. At this age, you just have to get through it. It's hard. And it's hard for *everybody*."

After I empathized with her, I reinforced all her wonderful qualities, her beauty and spirit, all the gifts she has. And then I gave her some suggestions for how to make friends. She's happy again and has a ton of friends now. That was an emotionally gut-wrenching experience for me but I knew she didn't need me falling apart on her. She needed my strength and support. Somehow I came through. Thank God."

Mothers have a wealth of wisdom when it comes to helping their daughters mend a broken heart. They shared their experiences and ideas.

Straight Talk from Moms

★ *Boys haven't broken my daughter's heart, but her dad has. My ex-husband can be verbally and emotionally abusive at times. I believe that whenever you have a divorce situation, it's in your child's best interest never to say anything negative about the other person. Sometimes it's really, really hard. I hold this image in my head that helps me stick to that rule. I know that if I ever say anything negative about her father to her, I'll be carving a little piece off her heart. At the same time, I want to empathize with the pain she feels about the way he treats her sometimes, but without bad-mouthing him about all the same ways he mistreated me. I just have to listen and listen, and listen some more. One thing we do is some mental imagery. When she's really hurting, she sees herself in a safe and loving place being totally loved. It's a tool she has used since she was little to take care and comfort herself.*

★ *I tell her, "Sometimes in the pain, there's a gift. Something you can learn." I've found that to be true in my own life, and it's been helpful to pass that on to her.*

★ *When something has hurt my daughter tremendously, I ask her to tell me the situation and exactly what happened. Tears always come up and I hold her. I rub her back for a while and let her cry. Eventually we'll talk and I'll ask her, "What would you have liked to have happened? Let's talk about what you'll do if it happens again."*

★ *I try and help my daughter become pro-active about her problems instead of passive. I want her to know there are a lot of different ways to get through a loss. I think she's naturally more optimistic as a result. At least I hope so.*

★ *The first thing I do when my daughter's heart is hurting is to try and relate to her stories. I might talk about something similar that happened to me. I empathize with her but only to a point, because then I'm going to try and lift her up and over the hurdle. I want to boost her up and out of the hole emotionally. So after some time I will say, "Okay, what are we going to do to get beyond this? It may take time, but you have to start here." From there we problem-solve and move on. I never want my daughter to believe that you have to get stuck in anything. There's always a way through any situation no matter how dark and dismal it may get.*

★ *My daughters are different. One is not as emotional or touchy-feely as the other one is. They had totally different ways of dealing with the death of their grandfather. I've had to learn why they're like that. They have different personalities, and so I need to help them differently. One clings and the other moves on. I tell them it's okay for them to have very different responses.*

★ *My daughter sees her feelings as unique rather than universal. I constantly remind her that she isn't the only one who has struggled with a broken heart and feelings of rejection. Teens need to know that pain is a part of life, and it's a part they can have some control over. At least in the way they respond to it.*

EMOTIONAL NEEDS

Every day is a new opportunity for your daughter to feel emotionally fulfilled, neutral, or depleted. The success she has at meeting her emotional needs is likely to depend on what's happening within herself, her home, and her environment or community.

Strengths and Resources

Personal strengths, family strengths, and community influences can all assist teens facing emotional troubles. Helping your daughter recognize and fortify her resiliency and sense of hope begins by identifying her strengths and resources.

Exercise: Identifying Her Strengths and Resources

Think about the following ways you might help strengthen your daughter's resiliency and sense of hope. Write down your responses and share them with your daughter to get her ideas and feedback.

Make a list of your daughter's personal strengths, including:

★ personality traits

★ academic successes

★ talents

★ special abilities

★ ways she is competent and successful in life

★ values and beliefs

Make a list of your daughter's strengths as they relate to your family life, describing:

★ the qualities of her primary parent figure(s)

★ her extended family support

★ her home atmosphere

List the strengths of the community in which your daughter lives, including:

★ positive adult relationships she enjoys outside your family

★ social organizations she participates in (for example, clubs, temple, church)

- ★ supportive friends who are important to her
- ★ positive qualities of the neighborhood she lives in
- ★ positive qualities found in the school she attends and the teachers she has

Almost every aspect of your daughter's life can play a significant role in developing her sense of competency. The more competent your daughter feels, the more she will be able to manage crises, feelings of distress, and any emotional challenges she faces.

Life Perspectives

Having a sense of humor and a meaningful spiritual life can also contribute to a healthy emotional life. Both offer perspectives on a life situation that may help build your daughter's resiliency and sense of hope.

A Sense of Humor

Happiness is contagious. One of the most effective coping skills you can encourage and help your daughter develop is a healthy sense of humor. Being able to laugh will decrease anxiety, stress, fear, anger, and depression. Here's what one teenage girl shared about humor: "I used to scream and yell and slam my door, like temper tantrums, but I don't do that anymore when I'm upset. I just run into my room and jump on my bed! It's so stupid that it makes me laugh." Another girl said:

> As I've gotten older I've found a silly way to handle my bad moods. I go up to my room and make fun of things, and then I feel better. I'm serious! I like putting magazine pictures up all over my walls and shouting out things to all the rich and famous stars. And then I go downstairs and I'm happy again. You probably think that's so weird, but it makes me laugh when I'm having a bad day.

The mother of a fifteen-year-old daughter offered this:

> My daughter mopes when she's unhappy and blames everyone else for her problems. I ask her, "Who's responsible for your happiness?" Inevitably she says, "How about you?" And I answer, "Not my job!" I think she used to believe my sole purpose in life was to make her happy. So now I just laugh, we joke about it, and I don't take on stuff I shouldn't.

A sense of humor will help both you and your daughter distance yourselves from your emotions. It also gives you the time and space to be more objective about the situation at hand. Don't be afraid to use humor in the midst of pain. As long as you are laughing *with* your daughter, not *at* her, and your humor is respectfully given and received, you will enjoy a bounty of benefits.

A Spiritual Life

You may want to consider packing a moral compass and a spiritual anchor (that weigh nothing) in your daughter's bags before she embarks on her journey to complete independence. Many teens seem eager to deepen their spiritual lives as a way of experiencing increased comfort and emotional support. Research has shown that teens who participate in religious organizations have lower levels of stress (Weaver et al. 1998; Garbarino 1999). Having a spiritual life and faith can be an important resource for teens. Religious faith itself can be psychologically protective because it provides structure to life and helps youth deal with worldly problems (Coles 1990; Hyde 1990).

Celia Straus found that sharing her love, support, and encouragement with her daughters was especially effective when written in prayers (Straus 1998). Prayer is particularly effective because when you pray you listen to your own inner voice and can find comfort from the fact that you are not alone or isolated (Levine 1999). Encouraging and providing the opportunity for your daughter to grow in her beliefs will be an added resource she can depend on in times of emotional turmoil.

The best way to convey your values and beliefs is through the example you set and follow. Live by what you say.

WARNING SIGNS

Some emotional problems require professional attention and aid. Even the most skilled, qualified, and loving mother can't possibly prevent or heal every wound. Significant depression and suicidal thoughts, feelings, or acts; prolonged grief; and anxiety disorders are serious emotional difficulties that require outside assistance. A psychiatrist or specialist in mental health care treatment can conduct an assessment and evaluation for appropriate medications, if necessary.

The following descriptions will give you some ideas of what to watch for, but remember that every situation is different.

Suicide and Depression

Profound depression in adolescence can lead to suicidal thoughts and feelings, especially in girls. Serious depression can be hard to recognize because it often seems like a normal passing phase of adolescence. Research from many nations has found that suicidal ideation, or thinking about suicide, is so common among high school students that it might be considered normal (Diekstra 1995). Seriously depressed teens often feel misunderstood and alone. Many believe their parents ignore them when they attempt to communicate their troubled feelings. Others feel they are never taken seriously.

Statements like the following by teenage girls are examples of a depressed spirit: "I heard about someone who cut herself to feel better. I tried it once. Nobody knows I did it. Sometimes I still do." "I don't care about anything anymore." "I think about ways I could die, so then everyone would be sorry and miss me." "I think about killing myself when I'm depressed because I'm tired of feeling this way." "I want to just disappear."

It is important for every parent to remain alert for the signs and symptoms of serious depression in teens. Take indications of a problem seriously. Keep in mind that whenever you're feeling concerned or puzzled about any unusual behavior your daughter exhibits, it is time to address it. Don't delay.

Look and Listen for These Signs:

★ a sudden drop in grades; educational pressure

★ personality change

★ chronic, sustained depression

★ alcohol and/or other drug use

★ fits of rage; frustration

★ loneliness, social rejection, loss of interest in social relationships

★ any form of self-destructive or deliberate acts of self-harm

★ extreme emotional agitation and confusion

★ noticeable changes in eating or sleeping habits

★ low energy and extreme fatigue

★ increased physical complaints, such as stomachaches, headaches, and backaches.

- ★ running away

- ★ persistent boredom and/or difficulty concentrating

- ★ neglect of appearance

- ★ a focus on themes of death

- ★ giving away prized possessions

- ★ jokingly making plans or talking about suicide

- ★ threatening or attempting to kill herself

Signs and symptoms in your adolescent may have been evident for a long time or not present at all. Girls have committed suicide who seemed happy, well-adjusted, and high achieving. They had learned to effectively hide their unhappiness and depression, even though it was so great that the only solution they saw was to end their life. Staying closely involved in your daughter's life will help you stay in touch with her state of mind. If you are concerned, you can take some of the following actions.

- ★ Talk to your daughter if you have any concerns about her emotional well-being.

- ★ Be honest. Tell her why you are concerned about her.

- ★ Ask her directly if she is thinking about hurting or killing herself.

- ★ Ask if she has made a plan.

- ★ Listen and take everything she says seriously. Assume any threat is real.

- ★ Give her hope. Tell her that with treatment, depression can end. Remind her that everyone feels sad or depressed at times and that she has important reasons for feeling the way she does.

- ★ Get help. A professional can diagnose your daughter's illness and determine a proper treatment plan.

If there's a problem, don't wait for it to "go away." Don't assume that your daughter's problems are solved just because her sadness and depression may seem to disappear quickly. She may still be at high risk. Remember, with professional treatment and support from family and friends, adolescent girls who are suicidal can become healthy again. Obtain help and support for yourself, too. Get phone numbers of local suicide hot lines, crisis centers, and mental health centers.

Prolonged Grief

When grieving becomes "complicated," it can prevent your daughter from resolving her sorrow. She may be unable to mourn in ways that will help her move on from an experience of loss. It can be difficult to tell if your daughter is grieving normally or not, because the intensity of her symptoms is *not* an indicator. Normal grieving typically involves a propensity for quick rage, intense anguish, and gripping fear. Consequently, it is difficult for parents to differentiate between what's normal and what has become a complicated bereavement in need of professional help.

Look and Listen for These Signs

★ irrational beliefs

★ denial of reality

★ fixations that prevent or postpone mourning

What Action to Take

★ Listen and let your daughter vent many times.

★ Let her release the full range of her emotions.

★ Let her talk out all her memories associated with the loss.

★ Don't give advice, correction, or judgment.

★ Respect her way of coming to terms with the loss.

★ Seek professional help or consultation if you have questions or concerns about your daughter's behaviors.

★ Remember, your daughter could be at risk for serious depression and suicide following the death of a family member or friend. Don't hesitate to find support for her if her grief becomes too great.

Anxiety Disorders

There are a host of anxiety disorders that can prove to be debilitating to teenage girls. If your daughter is suffering from anxiety that is incapacitating, she is likely to feel a great deal of shame and embarrassment. It may be difficult for her to talk about her symptoms, even though her anxiety is likely to be unbearable at times. Like many adults, adolescent girls may worry they are going "crazy" when they suffer from anxiety. Some fear they are even going to die, the physical symptoms can be so frightening.

When persistent feelings of anxiety prevent your daughter from enjoying life, realizing her potential, dreams, and goals, seek help. Anxiety can be successfully treated, and it happens to people of all ages. Your daughter needs to know she is not crazy or going crazy when symptoms overwhelm her.

Look and Listen for These Signs

★ intense and unrealistic fear associated with objects or situations

★ intense and irrational apprehension and fear

★ panic attacks

★ irrational fears of being humiliated or embarrassed

★ separation anxiety

★ avoidance behaviors

★ reexperiencing a traumatic life event

What Action to Take:

★ Share your concerns with your daughter.

★ Ask about her symptoms and normalize what she is experiencing.

★ Give empathetic understanding.

★ Give her unconditional acceptance and nonjudgmental responses.

★ Assure her that help is available and she does not have to continue to suffer. She can learn to manage and overcome her anxiety with the help of a professional who has special training and expertise in treating anxiety.

★ Find a counselor or therapist whom your daughter can trust.

★ Be patient. Progress can be slow and inconsistent at times.

★ Build up your daughter's self-esteem

★ Offer encouragement

★ Support a healthy regimen of sleep, nutrition, exercise, recreation, vacations, relaxation techniques, and even occasional breaks during the school week.

STRETCHING EXERCISES

The following exercises will help increase your daughter's emotional awareness and resiliency in the face of changing moods and feelings.

Exercise: Charting the Course

★ Give your daughter a calendar she can use daily to keep track of changing physical symptoms and moods.

★ Encourage her to use simple and fun symbols that will quickly identify her feelings. For example, she might use arrows pointing up or down to represent a high or low day, a heart to represent "love is in the air," an "X" to mark angry days, etc.

★ Watch for patterns and themes that emerge over several months. Being able to anticipate emotional changes will help your daughter take some control and empower her. Awareness and understanding can increase self-acceptance and lead to greater self-control.

Exercise: My Accepted and Denied List

★ On a piece of paper make two columns. Title the first one "Accepted Emotions." List only those emotions that you welcome, enjoy, and can express fully and comfortably.

★ Title the second column "Denied Emotions." List those feelings that you dread, feel uncomfortable about, push away, or avoid expressing.

★ Ask your daughter to figure out what your columns include. Then share your responses with her.

★ Ask her to complete the same lists. Try and figure out what her columns will include and ask her to share her responses if she's willing.

Exercise: Emotional Scaling

On a scale of 1 to 10, ask your daughter to identify the number that best describes her current emotional state (one being as sad as she could ever feel and ten being ecstatically happy). Ask her what made her choose the number she did and what would need to happen to change it. Where was she on the scale yesterday? Why? Where would she like to be tomorrow? What does she need to do to get there? Are her expectations realistic? Why or why not? (You may want to encourage her to improve her number in some small way, rather than trying to attain a major change.)

Talk with her about where *you* are on the scale and where you would like to be tomorrow.

Exercise: Prayer Journal

Start a prayer journal with your daughter that you pass back and forth. Write personalized prayers for her. Leave spaces for her to list "prayer requests" after each entry. As a matter of routine, exchange the prayer journal between you each day.

Exercise: Climbing Out of Depression

Sit down and write out your thoughts as you respond to the following questions:

1. Based on your personal experiences, what can you teach your daughter about defeating depression?

2. Based on your personal experiences, what can you teach your daughter about where she can find hope? Where can you direct her?

CHAPTER 5

Her Emerging Sexuality

Tonight was the best night of my life. I danced four slow dances and two of them were with Taylor! He is so buff and so sweet. The first dance he held me around my waist, which was very sexy. But the second dance he pulled me in nice and close. He held me against him really tight and my whole body totally melted into his. I loved it! Okay, then at the end was the best part. He put his head down on my shoulder and kissed my neck!! I almost fainted! He is so sexy! I can't wait until there's a chance to be alone with him. Hope it's soon.

—Diary entry from a fourteen-year-old girl

From the moment puberty begins, adolescent girls are likely to become interested in sex. Attraction, physical pleasure, and love all spark new and exciting sensations. Pleasure, intimacy, and sexual desire are compelling drives that ultimately result in three decisions your daughter will face: what kind of sexual activity she will engage in, when she will do it, and with *whom*.

Most mothers feel anxious anticipating the outcome of such decisions. They also feel anxious about the boys who may become interested in their daughters. The mother of a fifteen-year-old fresh-man walked into her daughter's high school for the first time and had this reaction: "I realized my 'little girl' is now in this huge school with older, 210-pound guys with facial hair! And I just thought to myself, 'You just stay away from my daughter!' I want her to go in there with security guards and a chastity belt. I'm nervous! Right now she's conservative in her views about sex, but realistically I know that could all change very quickly."

Another mother told her discussion group: "We have to remember that boys are at an age now when they want to experiment with girls," to which another mom responded, "It's an age they never get out of." The group jokingly agreed that much of what their daughters will learn in adolescence would be true for the rest of their lives.

Many girls never tell their mothers about sexual matters related to their feelings or relationships with others. Your daughter may share your values or depart from them, without you ever knowing. Not all girls become sexually active in their teen years or have a diffi-cult time coping with their sexual lives; nevertheless, it is essential to teach adolescent girls everything. The best choices can only be made when teens are fully informed and have a clear understanding of all the physical and emotional ramifications of their decisions.

Not only does an effective education about sexuality encompass all the facts; it includes the teaching of important beliefs and values pertaining to sex. The best way to influence your daughter is to talk to her about your beliefs and openly explain your reasons for them.

Regardless of whether or not your daughter engages in conver-sations with you about sex, the only way you can hope to influence her choices is by communicating with her about it. Be ready to artic-ulate and explain your views and values in order to give your daughter more than "just the facts" to guide her and help her work out her own values. You can also:

✦ Encourage her to develop attitudes and social skills that will help her refrain from sexual intercourse until she has gained enough maturity to understand and take responsi-bility for the consequences.

✦ Be able to articulate what you believe are appropriate behav-iors to engage in at her age and what behaviors are not.

✦ If possible, encourage your daughter's father to share his views, too. A male perspective that supports a positive and respectful view of women's sexuality can be a compelling example and message to her.

Establish your influence by sharing your beliefs and values, guide your daughter with education, and then give her unconditional love and support no matter what. You don't have to agree with your daughter's behavior, and being honest and direct about that is important. But shaming her for behaviors you don't approve of will only drive a wider wedge between you.

When you can uphold an attitude of acceptance, and speak to all the facets of your daughter's emerging sexuality with openness and honesty, you will provide her with what she needs in order to make sound decisions during this period of her development. You will also be pointing her in the right direction on the path to a lifetime of sexual health and fulfillment.

SHAME OR CELEBRATION

Your daughter's attitude about her emerging sexuality plays a significant role in how she feels about herself. The visible changes your daughter sees on the outside and the inner changes she feels on the inside affect her ability to welcome or deny her emerging sexuality.

Acceptance, embarrassment, pride, and shame are powerful reactions that can result from any number of factors. Cultural conditions may influence a teen's thinking. A family's belief system may encourage or discourage sexual awareness and experimentation, and peer groups often exert influence on a teen's sexual attitudes and behaviors. A girl's sense of pride can increase when she is well informed, and when the guidance and education she receives is presented in a positive light.

It's normal and healthy for girls to have a strong need for privacy around sexuality issues. The need to protect privacy is appropriate and necessary for healthy maturation. Most girls don't care to discuss the specifics of their experiences with their moms or, to some extent, even with their friends. Even though this is normal, it can make the process of helping your daughter especially difficult. Mothers sometimes feel at a loss for how to guide, educate, and influence their teen's newfound sexual awareness. Consequently, some mothers do not step up to the plate, and the job gets passed on to someone else.

GO ASK YOUR SISTER

A number of parents seem to do a good job of educating their adolescent daughters about sex. However, most girls receive their information from peers, siblings, or other sources.

A woman who was the youngest sister of three shared this story about her mother's involvement in one aspect of her sex education:

There was a pool party I really wanted to go to when I was thirteen, but I was on my period. I was so anxious to go that I asked my mother about tampons, or "plugs" as my two sisters called them. I had never used one before, but I was motivated to learn. I stood around hemming and hawing and finally asked her, "Well, where do you put them? Will I still be able to go to the bathroom? Where does it plug in?" She just said, "Go ask your sister!"

So I did. Both of my sisters ended up coaching me. They handed me a tampon, shut the bathroom door, and started yelling through the crack of it, "Lift up your leg!" "Push it in at an angle!" "Put your finger in first!" "Keep it at an angle!" "Point it toward your back!" This went on for about a half hour. I didn't have the slightest idea what I was doing or where the tampon was supposed to be going. Consequently it went nowhere. I decided to skip the pool party rather than continue the torture. My mom never said another word and I never asked another question.

Mothers are sometimes awkward about explaining sex and uninformed about how to best go about it. They fear knowledge will lead to experimentation, or it will be too much for their daughters to handle. A woman shared the following story about the way her mother approached her about sexual matters when she was in early adolescence:

My mom came in my room one day and sat down next to me on my bed. She seemed a little tense and way too serious. Then she solemnly asked me, "Do you know what masturbation is? Your sister thought I should talk to you about it." "Oh yeah! I know all about that," I proudly replied. She looked surprised and asked nervously, "Well, what does it mean?"

With confident authority, I explained, "That's when you start growing hair under your armpits, get B.O., and start developing boobs." My mother sat silent for a few moments and then in an upbeat sort of way said, "Okay." She quickly left my room and never said another word to me about anything sexual again.

A couple of years later I came across the word "masturbation" in a magazine article. When I looked up the meaning, I was flabbergasted. I was instantly humbled by my ignorance. Convinced there was probably still more I was in the dark about, I began searching through all the sex books I could get my hands on—many of which we're not clear representations of healthy sexuality but were the only sources available to me. I had a lot to unlearn when I got older. I decided then and there it would be so much easier to have someone you trust give you the right information from the start. So, that's what I do for my daughter. Either I educate her or someone else will. I choose *me*.

Many moms want their daughters to remain innocent; others feel ill-equipped and lack the confidence to instruct them. But when girls lack accurate and clear information about their bodies and sexuality, their mothers do a disservice to them. Not only do they lack important information; they get the message that for some reason the subject is off-limits. Most girls conclude this means that there is something wrong or bad about their questions and about the whole subject of sex. Fear and confusion are the result.

Your daughter can benefit from your knowledge and experience. She needs your support to survive the teen years and beyond. She also gains trust and reassurance when she knows she can depend on you to guide her confidently through all the phases of her development.

PREPARE YOURSELF

It's important to prepare yourself for talking about sex before you prepare your daughter. A mother shared an incident that made her realize it was time to start preparing her thirteen-year-old daughter for relating to guys:

> My daughter and I were at the community pool one afternoon when she happened to say in passing how some guy asked her out. "Asked you *out*?" I asked. "What do you mean?" She told me, "Well, you talk, go out, break up, and then never see him again." I got home and thought, "Hmm. Do I need to talk to her more about sex and boys?" I was just shocked. I realized it might be time to prepare her a little more, but I had to stop and try to figure out what to say. It doesn't come as easily as I always expected it to. I wasn't prepared.

Set Your Goals

There are a number of ideas and goals to consider before you begin or continue the process of educating your daughter about sex.

Don't ignore the fact that your daughter is growing into a sexual young woman, but be careful not to put her sexuality in the spotlight either. Know that experimentation is not uncommon with members of the same or opposite sex. Also, remember that girls who take pleasure and pride in their own developing bodies are more likely to accept sexual desire as natural, not shameful.

What You Can Do

★ Appreciate her sexual maturation in the same way you appreciate other aspects of her growth and development.

★ Help her understand the changes taking place in her body. She needs to know that everyone matures at his or her own rate.

★ Keep your conversations with your daughter plain and simple. Avoid long lectures and endless details. Answer what she needs to know and skip the long illustrations and stories unless she wants to hear them.

★ Look for opportunities to educate her. Be open and ready for spontaneous occasions when you can share information.

Know the Facts

★ Make sure your information and knowledge about sex is current and accurate. Be prepared to:

★ Give her the facts about conception, pregnancy, and childbirth.

★ Describe the mechanics of sex. Remember, it does require some explaining.

★ Explain the process of human sexual response and expression. Include a conversation about orgasm and masturbation.

★ Explain contraception and how to prevent pregnancy. Remind her that both sexes must take responsibility for preventing pregnancy and disease.

★ Educate her about sexually transmitted diseases (STDs) and their prevention.

★ Help your daughter understand the importance of routine exams with a gynecologist once she becomes sexually active.

You won't be able to teach your daughter everything at once. Sex education is an ongoing process that takes place over a period of time and in a variety of different ways. Judge what information is either critical for her to know now or is of interest to her, and begin there. Remember, this is a time of life that requires a lot of understanding. Prepare yourself, so you are better able to help your daughter deal with common changes and potential problems related to her sexual development.

SEXUAL HEALTH ISN'T JUST PHYSICAL

Sexual health isn't just physical; it's emotional and psychological, too. Help your daughter understand that sex can be acted on in a way that honors her values, goals, and her significant other.

The Emotional Risks

You can tell her that sexual activity is enhanced when it is based on esteem, commitment, and respect, but let her know that even sexual activity with commitment can be risky for teenage girls.

What You Might Say

★ "With a sexual relationship comes an emotional intensity and bonding that can be difficult to handle."

★ "Breaking up from a relationship that you've been sexually involved in is more emotionally draining and can even lead to depression and suicide in some girls."

★ "If you avoid breaking off an unhealthy relationship because you are sexually involved, it may restrict you from realizing your personal growth."

★ "When teens are in sexually active relationships, often friendships, academics, individual talents, and interests are curtailed, with negative consequences."

★ "Early sexual relationships, with or without commitment, cause many adolescent girls more emotional and social complications than they can usually handle."

TEACHING ABSTINENCE

There are a number of reasons why abstinence, refraining from sexual intercourse, is an option teenagers should consider. One is it prevents pregnancy. Another is it eliminates the risk of contracting human immunodeficiency virus (HIV), acquired immunodeficiency syndrome (AIDS), hepatitis B, hepatitis C, and other sexually transmitted diseases.

Some girls have vowed to wait to have sex because of their values and belief systems. For whatever reason they choose abstinence, doing so can allow teenage girls the extra time they need to mature in all aspects of their development. Many teens believe waiting to have sex until they're older is a good idea. A sixteen–year-old girl said this:

> Well, I know a lot of people don't think I can do it, but I really want to wait until I'm older to worry about a sexual relationship. There's a lot to deal with already and throwing sex into my life now would really make it hard. I don't want to worry about birth control and abortion and AIDS. I can't think about that stuff right now. I have enough to do without all that. I might change my mind when I get out of high school, but I really want it to be with the right person, so who knows when that will be? So far, every guy I've thought was "the one" has turned out not to be. So I don't want to do anything until I'm sure.

Making the Choice to Wait

Abstinence can become an option at any point during your daughter's sexual development. She may decide it's a decision she wants to make, whether or not she's already engaged in sexual activity.

What You Can Do

★ Explain that abstinence is a practical and viable choice your daughter can make about her sexuality.

★ Explain that abstinence is not the same as repression. The decision to abstain from sex is a choice made based on sound reasons, not from a sense of fear or shame.

★ Recommend that your daughter list all the pros and cons of choosing abstinence on a piece of paper.

★ Ask her what skills she can use that will help her resist social and peer pressures to have early sex.

★ If she chooses to make this commitment to herself, ask what would be important to her success.

Safe Self-Expression

If your daughter tells you she has made the decision to abstain from sexual activity throughout adolescence, it's important to support her choice with confidence. But keep in mind that normal sexual adjustment for teens involves learning to relate to others who they find romantically and physically attractive. Finding a balance somewhere between sexual permissiveness and sexual repression is important. Even if she doesn't appear interested in the idea, it's possible to help your daughter find a healthy balance of behaviors that can allow for growth, learning, and safe experimentation.

Not all daughters will want to tell their mothers about the choices they are making or planning to make. Many don't know what choices they'll make from day to day, let alone throughout the rest of their teen years. But regardless of how open and forthright your daughter is or isn't about sexual matters, it's still important to talk about the value of healthy and safe self-expression. In other words, you can teach your daughter that safe self-expression means enjoying intimacy without the sex.

Your daughter needs to know that it's possible for girls to abstain from sexual relations and still enjoy their emerging sexuality in safe and pleasurable ways. Like other limits and structure you provide for your daughter, you can offer guidelines for what safe parameters for self-expression are. For example, you might talk to her about the value of kissing, holding hands, hugging, dancing, massage, and tender touch that is not intended to lead to intercourse. You could explain that closeness is enjoyable even with all your clothes on.

It is natural for your daughter to want to share private time with someone she cares for deeply. Helping her identify early on what she will and will not participate in can prepare her for the choices she will face and help her avoid entering into a physical relationship before she is ready. At the same time, she will be acquiring an understanding of the wide range of behaviors that can safely communicate love, caring, and commitment without going "all the way."

THE BIG "M" WORD

Like many aspects of adolescent sexuality, a number of girls aren't sure what to think about masturbation because they haven't been told what to think about it. Others have been told it is a sin, it is addictive, or it is okay for boys but strange and unusual behavior for girls. Girls may worry and wonder if it's okay to have enjoyable thoughts about sex or if, in fact, they are engaging in shameful pre-occupations when they do so.

A guilt-ridden fifteen-year-old came into my office one morning. She shared the following account:

> I'm still a virgin and everything, but I don't want you to think less of me. I'm so ashamed to tell you this. I . . . think I might have a problem. I asked, "A problem related to sex?" "Not really sex. But I don't know, maybe." I continued to explore, "Can you tell me why you think that?" "Because of what I'm doing," she answered. "Well, whatever it is you're doing, I can guarantee you're not the only one. Almost every teenager wonders if they're normal sexually." She continued, "I'm afraid you'll think I'm terrible." I asked her if she could think of a way to tell me that wouldn't be so embarrassing. She looked down on her shoes and quietly said, "I'm not doing it with anyone, but I still do it." "Oh," I said nonchalantly, "are you talking about masturbation?" She lifted her head just far enough for me to see the shell-shocked expression on her face and mouth gaping open. From the stunned look on her face, I wondered for a split second if I had guessed wrong. I waved my hand in front of her bulging eyes and said, "Hey, you look like your sitting on death row instead of in my office!" And then as fast as she could, she said, "I know it's really bad, but I did it once and now I know why everyone likes sex so much! I'm afraid I have a problem because now I like it, too. I try not to do it too much, but I haven't stopped it. Do you think I'm awful?"
>
> "Do I think you're awful for discovering that your body responds as it's supposed to when it's been sexually stimulated?" I said. "Of course not. All your parts are in working order. That's a good thing to know." "Really?" she asked, in relief and disbelief. "Yes, really. That's the way I see it. And quite frankly I think there are some advantages to exploring your sexuality alone for now."

She asked me if I thought she could be addicted to it. I explained that in my opinion there's a healthy way and unhealthy way to do almost everything in life, including sex. Sexual activity, like any behavior, can become a means of self-medicating pain and stress. If it becomes compulsive and serves as an escape for other problems, it could become addictive. I told her I didn't think that was the case in her situation, but that we'd keep talking and figure it out.

It's not uncommon for girls to associate their sexual desires with something in them they think must be "unusual" or "sick." Masturbation can arouse feelings of anxiety, guilt, and the belief that it might be abnormal, or harmful. A fifteen-year-old girl told me:

> So I was talking to a friend on the phone one night, and she said I should try fingering myself. I was like, "What? Are you some kind of a pervert or something? Only horny guys do that!" Like, seriously, I thought maybe she had a problem or something. But after we hung up, I ended up trying it . . . the big "M" word. I liked it and I'm trying not to ever do it again, but it's hard not to! I feel so bad. Am I sick and twisted or what?

Adolescent girls need to be told that masturbation is a very normal part of human sexual functioning, and is widely practiced. Medical doctors, psychologists, and clergy from a variety of faith backgrounds agree that masturbation can be a safe and healthy way to release sexual energy.

Most girls won't want to discuss this issue with their mothers, but you can still provide them with the information they need to understand their potential concerns. One woman told me how she used her dog, Sundance, to help educate her daughter about the sex drive and privacy issues:

> Our mellow, friendly, calm retriever is sweet as can be. She never gives us a bit of trouble. She just has this one thing. This habit. Whenever a blanket or pillow hits the ground, she jumps it and furiously humps it to shreds. She's been spayed, but you'd think she was in heat or on Viagra by the looks of her. We were standing in the utility room the first time my daughter and I witnessed this together. I made a "not this again" kind of facial expression and my daughter went into a fit of laughter.
>
> Then I went into a lecture mode with the dog and said, "Now, Sundance, we understand you have a sex drive like anyone else, and masturbation isn't harmful, but you

need to practice some modesty. You're out of control! You need to masturbate in the privacy of your own room and not share it with anyone, including us! We'd appreciate it if you wouldn't use our linens for your self-gratification in the future." Ever since that happened, my daughter and I have been able to talk more comfortably about sexual information. It helped. Let's face it, sometimes it's easier to talk to a dog than it is a teen. I say use whatever way you can to teach and communicate about sex.

Not all teenage girls are embarrassed to talk about masturbation or, for that matter, any aspect of their sexuality. A sixteen-year-old girl told me:

I grew up knowing it all. I mean what's the big deal talking about sex and masturbation and getting off? Hey, I'd rather masturbate than do it with a loser or get myself pregnant, or some disease. I'm not so pathetic that masturbation is my life you know, but we all do it, so why the big secret and why be all hush-hush about it? It's stupid! I get tired of all that bullshit. Just talk about it. I don't care who knows.

RISKY SEX

An understanding of the basic facts of sexuality is no guarantee that teenage girls will see the wisdom in abstaining from sex or in practicing responsible and safe sex. Engaging in risky sexual behaviors is a common experience for many teens. Some say it gives them status, a feeling of personal power, helps them make friends, and is a way to have fun. Teens are especially good at disconnecting their minds from their behavior. When it serves them to do so, they can set aside their values.

Even when adolescents engage in risky behaviors that prove to be a mistake, they don't always learn from the experience. After she had completed a pregnancy prevention class a sixteen-year-old girl told me: "I'm pregnant again. I can't believe this happened. I thought if you got pregnant once, you were safe. I didn't think you could be unlucky twice, so I didn't bother to take the birth control pills the clinic gave me."

Irrational Thinking

Adolescent girls are only beginning to develop the reasoning skills they need to make mature decisions. They often exhibit irrational thinking and errors in judgment because of the vulnerability of this stage in their life. Decision-making in the area of sexual behavior can be especially unpredictable.

When making choices about sex, girls often have difficulty envisioning alternatives and they tend to focus only on immediate considerations. The long-term consequences of pregnancy, abortion, and parenthood are inconvenient to think about and, for many, it doesn't seem realistic to think about anyway.

What You Can Do

★ Become more rational in *your* thinking.

★ Explain to your daughter why she might be at risk for acting on impulsive decisions and behaviors.

★ Talk about ways she can minimize the risks. Encourage her to think and plan ahead. Help her to visualize how she could handle risky situations in a positive way.

★ Whether your beliefs and values encourage or discourage the teaching of birth control methods to teens, remember that their health and safety may depend on understanding the range of protection that can be used, not just to prevent pregnancy, but to prevent the spread of HIV and other diseases. Imparting your beliefs and values, combined with prevention education, can empower your daughter to make healthy decisions. If she doesn't feel comfortable talking to you about it, take her to her doctor or a family planning clinic for help.

★ Show her the consequences of risky behavior. Let her hear firsthand about the experiences of others. You might want to contact speakers for your daughter's class, youth group, or club who would be willing to contribute their time to help adolescents learn from their own life experiences. (For example, an HIV-positive teen or adult, a teen mother, a teen or an adult with herpes, hepatitis B, etc.)

Having His Baby

Many sexually active adolescents believe it is unlikely they will become pregnant after just one experience. Girls may believe they can't get pregnant for a number of erroneous reasons, which increases their risk-taking behaviors. These are a few of the explanations I have heard from sexually active teens:

★　"I just believe I'm sterile. I don't know why."

★　"I just have the feeling I'll never be able to have a baby. I just know there's something that's probably wrong and I won't be able to."

★　"My mom had a hard time getting pregnant, so I'm sure I will, too."

★　"I can't get pregnant because I have irregular periods."

★　"I don't feel any eggs in my ovaries."

★　"I don't orgasm."

★　"My boyfriend pulls out his penis as quick as he can."

★　"I just had a baby, so we're safe for a while."

★　"I always pee really fast after we do it, so all the sperm is rinsed out."

★　"He keeps his penis on the outside of me. He doesn't go in."

★　"We only did it once."

Few teen girls try to become pregnant, but if they do get pregnant and if they decide to keep the baby, most don't think it will be so bad. A pregnant teen is usually more worried about what her parents will do and whether the birth will be painful. Very few girls are able to look at long-range plans such as the day-to-day responsibilities of raising a child or preventing another pregnancy. Adolescent girls often say they believe a baby might make them happier, bring their relationship with their boyfriend closer, and that it will be fun to love and be loved by their baby. In fact, in most cases having a baby does not make them happier or improve their relationship with their boyfriend. Quite the opposite is true.

Research indicates that unwanted pregnancies slow teens' educational and vocational achievement and restrict social and personal growth. Employment and marriage are often delayed, and if girls marry because they're pregnant, they have a greater chance of being abused, abandoned, or eventually divorced (Harris and Furstenberg 1997). When unwanted pregnancies occur, the baby's health is also at greater risk, with a higher incidence of prenatal and birth complications as well as mistreatment (Fergusson and Woodward 1999).

You are your daughter's best resource for help and support. If she becomes pregnant, the understanding you give her is important. However, if pregnancy results from rape or incest, your daughter may feel unable to seek your help. She may be too ashamed, confused, embarrassed, or frightened to disclose her situation to you (see chapter 7 for more help regarding rape, incest, and sexual harassment). And some girls who are convinced they are pregnant actually aren't. They need practical help and medical attention to expand their thinking and information.

Having His STD

Adolescents need appropriate information about all the ways sexually transmitted diseases can be spread. Many teens mistakenly believe they aren't at risk for contracting diseases when they engage in oral stimulation or other behaviors that don't involve vaginal intercourse or complete penetration of the penis. Inform your daughter. Tell her exactly how STDs can be caught and how they may be prevented.

What You Can Say

★ STDs are spread by sexual contact, not just sexual intercourse. They can also be spread through same-sex relationships. Viruses can be spread by the mouth, sometimes the hands, and through genital contact, even when intercourse is not involved.

★ There is no cure for the HIV virus. Your risk increases when:

1. You or a partner are already infected with an STD.

2. You have more than one partner within a year.

3. You don't use condoms.

★ Hepatitis B, hepatitis C, venereal warts, herpes, chlamydia, syphilis, and gonorrhea are other dangerous STDs. While most can be treated promptly, there are no cures for some. Left untreated, all STDs can cause lifelong sterility and life-threatening complications. (It never hurts to show teens some up-close and personal pictures of a few warts and herpes sores.)

★ Venereal warts can be difficult to treat and are highly contagious. They can grow anywhere inside or outside the vagina and penis. They are contagious even when they have not grown large enough to be visible.

★ Herpes is also highly contagious, even when there are no visible signs of it. There is no cure. Most people live with painful outbreaks throughout their lives.

★ Latex condoms are the only contraceptive that can help prevent STDs.

It can be frightening and discouraging to learn about all the ways women can suffer from being sexual. While it's important that your daughter know the physical dangers of entering into a sexual relationship, it's also important to balance the negative with the positive. She deserves to know how sexuality can be practiced safely so that it can be an enjoyable experience throughout her life.

SEX SELLS

Your daughter also deserves to know the difference between fact and fiction in the media. Teenage girls are challenged not only by their own emerging sexuality but also by the culture's influence on their sexuality. A lot of mothers complain that "sex is everywhere." Many believe it has become a national obsession. Many mothers worry that the way sex is portrayed in the media will have a bad influence on their daughters' sexual development and health.

Straight Talk from Moms

★ *It's a market and it's driven by money. That's the bottom line. It's a business that is inundating our girls with damaging influences, impacting their self-esteem.*

★ *The more vulgar and shocking it is, the better it sells because it "hooks" people. Then people need even more vulgarity to be able to top the last shocking information they got. And so it continues, getting raunchier and raunchier.*

★ *My daughter becomes more accepting of the vulgar behaviors she sees on some of the talk shows. Our kids get desensitized to it. They think less about it when it appears to be everywhere.*

★ *When we see this stuff on television and the movies or hear it on the radio and on their CDs it's an opportunity to train them to be critical thinkers. They need to learn how to look at all sides of what they view and hear. We need to teach them how to listen and see differently.*

★ *The culture is such that teen issues are more like adult issues now. We have normalized abnormal behavior to the point that it can be confusing for kids to know what's okay and what's not. And of course the pressure to do what's not okay is going to impact some girls more than others.*

★ *To a certain extent you have to let your daughters see and experience what's in their culture, even the negative stuff. I was completely sheltered from it when I was growing up. I was not allowed to know what was going on in the real world. I think you do your children a great disservice by doing that. You have to let them figure it out while they're still with you. It's so much easier than having to figure it out as an adult by yourself.*

★ *I finally made myself listen to the music my daughters are hearing; there is horrible stuff out there. There is so much foul language that it makes them wonder if we're the only ones on the planet who don't use that language!*

★ *My daughters are more interested in television and magazines now. Even teen magazines are all about sexually suggestive topics. Our girls are subjected to so much more than we were.*

★ *My daughter wants to dress "trashier" than I ever did. Of course I had to dress like a little girl until I was married. I'm not kidding! So it does seem important to let her be a little more free to experiment with the way she dresses. I don't want her to look "trashy," but I do want her to enjoy her emerging femininity by the clothes she chooses. That seems healthy to me.*

★ *It's tough because on the one hand I tell my daughter it's not okay to look "sleazy," but I also don't want her to be ashamed of her body or sexuality. I think it's a confusing message sometimes.*

Many teenagers today are subjected to a steady diet of sexual messages that are often unreal and hurtful. The media portrays couples engaging in sex with little commitment and shows them in spontaneous and passionate encounters that look glamorous and romantic. As one mother stated, "Our kids are being spoon-fed a fantasy that is dangerous and confusing. Being teenagers, most will model their behaviors after what looks exciting, not what is rational."

It's clear that sex sells. Sexual messages can be seen or heard in almost every medium of entertainment, and these messages have grown more explicit, both verbally and visually. Still, there are some ways you can help your daughter approach the culture she finds herself in.

Pornography

First, it's important to have a discussion about pornography with your daughter, as she is increasingly exposed to language and pictures that violate, demean, and dishonor women and their sexuality. These are not the standards for behavior that most moms want their daughters to adopt.

When girls are bombarded by both soft and hard porn, they are learning that there are contrived looks, behaviors, and personas that are expected of women. The sooner you debunk these outrageous messages, the easier it will be to help your daughter accept her emerging sexuality with pride and self-respect. One mother said this: "When girls hit the teen years, their world just gets so much bigger so incredibly quickly. All of a sudden they're comparing themselves to beauty stars and supermodels. Their self-esteem can't help but plummet a bit. And that's just the nice stuff, not all the graphic sexual images they'll start getting exposed to."

When your daughter can accept herself for who she is, not whom she thinks she is supposed to be or must try and become, she gains valuable self-worth. Rather than alter her status, help her seek to beautify who she is instead. Self-acceptance is important to the development of a confident and pleasurable sense of sexuality.

What You Can Say

★ "Pornography can be harmful to all who view it."

★ "Pornography and sexual images in the media often misrepresent what the most important relationships in life are supposed to be like."

★ "Pornography and sexual images in the media can generate intense confusion as to what normal sexuality is."

★ "Women may compare themselves to the 'ideal woman' manufactured in the media and feel inadequate or inferior."

★ "Too much exposure to or dependency on pornography can end up in addiction and destroy a person's capacity for intimacy."

★ "When violence is associated with sex, it sends a dangerous and false message about the true meaning and purpose of sexuality."

- ✱ "Images, ideas, and words can leave a lasting and influential imprint on your thoughts and feelings."

Mothers have the sometimes daunting task of trying to figure out where and how to draw the line around what their teens are watching and listening to. It's difficult, if not impossible, to protect adolescents from all harmful influences. However, as a concerned mother, you can prepare your daughter for what she will see and then talk about the potential impact of what she sees and listens to. You can help her develop an antenna for detecting lies and misguided representations of what healthy sexuality is. By doing so, you are giving her an antidote for the sometimes dangerous and toxic messages she will receive.

PROMOTING HEALTHY SEXUALITY

Sexual desire is not a bad thing. In fact, it's a fun thing for most women. It's important for your daughter to hear this from you. She needs to know that women can enjoy a lifetime of satisfying and healthy sex. You may want to explain that when physical intimacy is combined with the joys of emotional intimacy it can be an experience most women say is unparalleled by any other.

The decision to have children adds a new dimension to sex. You may want to talk about how the meaning of sex changes, depending on your relationship with your partner. You can explain to your daughter that when love and sex are combined, the results are very different than when sex is purely a habit, compulsion, or a choice that's been entered into lightly.

Honoring Her Womanhood

By learning to honor her womanhood, your daughter is more likely to revere her sexuality and consider all her choices carefully. When you talk with her, emphasize the connection between sex, love, and commitment. Help her understand that real love and "lovemaking" involves a partner who not only loves her but thinks of her feelings and needs while having sex.

What You Can Say

- ✱ "Don't be afraid of sexual desire. Respect it. Sexual feelings, longings, and passions are fine and natural."

- ✱ "Your body has been designed to experience pleasure from sex. Once you are mature enough and have made the choice to become sexually active, it can be fun and enjoyable."

★ "Part of becoming a woman means learning how to control your sex drive."

★ "Part of maturity means you understand all the risks and consequences of any choice you make."

★ "Maturity also means you make choices that honor your views, beliefs, and values."

★ "You deserve to experience a sexual relationship that rests on a foundation of profound love, care, and commitment."

★ "Wait for the best experience you can have. Don't ever settle for less."

★ "Guard your heart. Wait to give the gift of your sexuality to the right person."

★ "Relationships don't have to be sexual to prove love or to be special."

★ "Relationships that are healthy will continue to be positive and lasting whether you're sexual or not."

If you hold religious beliefs and values about sex, be careful that you don't give the impression that sex is sinful. Clarify for her what your beliefs say about certain behaviors, not sex itself. Many girls agree with their moms that waiting to have sex until they're married is important and wise, not because sex is bad, but because sex is a special gift to be shared within the marital relationship. If possible, encourage your daughter's father to share his thoughts and views about healthy sexuality and the ways he has chosen to honor women.

WARNING SIGNS

Mothers naturally want to protect their daughters from unwise choices and risky behaviors, especially when those behaviors can be life altering or life threatening. Your daughter may be at risk for endangering herself if she is feeling pressured into sex, behaving in a sexually promiscuous way, or feeling emotionally troubled about sex.

The following signs will give you a general idea of what to watch for. Keep in mind that every situation is unique.

Pressured into Sex

Girls who have sex early in adolescence are typically pressured into doing so. Most girls say they are pressured routinely for sex when on dates. A sixteen-year-old girl described the following situation that she later regretted:

> Okay, you know I want to be a virgin when I get married, right? Well, I let Kevin "finger me" last night because he was like, "Oh please, I love you. It's not really sex." And every time I'm with him he's, like, all begging me to "Please, please do it with me ... I love you and would never hurt you." So finally I said okay, because I was curious, too. Plus I didn't want him to dump me. But then he kept begging me to keep doing it even though I didn't like it, because he said I just needed to keep trying. I didn't feel anything except it kind of hurt. I finally just said I didn't want to do this anymore. He said okay and was nice about it, but now I'm sorry I ever let him touch me. I feel like I let myself down.

Look and Listen for These Signs

★ feelings of shame or guilt

★ disappointment in someone

★ passing comments about feeling pressured, teased, or frustrated by someone

★ early physical maturation

★ others expecting her to act older than her age because of her looks

★ embarrassment about her physical development

★ feeling different, or as if something is wrong with her

★ anger with someone

★ avoidance, or not wanting to be with certain people or groups

What Action to Take

★ Ask your daughter directly if she has felt pressured into sexual activity.

★ Tell her that if sex is ever forced on her, it is rape and it is a crime. (See chapter 7.)

★ Tell her that her body is hers and she never has to give in to any pressure.

★ Remind her that she is perfectly capable of making up her own mind.

★ Explain that sex is never a way to say "thank you" for a date. If you are afraid of "losing him," you are at risk of losing your self-respect. Don't use sex to hold on to someone. It never works.

★ Help your daughter be prepared for how she will handle a situation in which she might be pressured to engage in sexual activity. Talk about flattering overtures and how she can be prepared to resist them.

★ Encourage her to think ahead about what her personal boundaries and limits are.

★ Help her practice what she can say and do to remain in control of her body and her choices.

★ Prepare her for how strong the sex drive can be, in herself and others. Let her know, that at times, she may be faced with situations that feel overwhelming. Practicing a way out in her mind ahead of time will help her act on it in reality.

★ Role-play some situations that might be hard for anyone to deal with.

Sexual Promiscuity

Sex can provide a means for some girls to feel loved, wanted, desired, and accepted. Sex may be the only way they feel valued and wanted. Some girls are so hungry for love and affection that they are willing to compromise their standards and own desires to please someone who wants to be with them. A sixteen-year-old girl told me:

> I've had sex with a lot of guys. I don't know why, I just do. It's not like I enjoy it. It's okay, but it's really the guy who enjoys it, not me. I feel like if I can't get them to have sex with me, then I'm not good enough for them, and then I get down on myself and go into a depression. I'm serious! I get really depressed if a guy doesn't want to have sex with me.

But I lose all my boyfriends because of it, too. I don't want to be called a "ho"; I just never want to stay with one guy. I don't know what is wrong with me. I want to change, but I don't know how.

Some girls say they don't feel guilty at all about "getting all they can." They want sex and don't really care about the other person's feelings. Promiscuous behavior can also be learned. Some girls learn that their only worth comes from a willingness to please others sexually.

Look and Listen for These Signs

★   a history of incest or sexual abuse

★   deep feelings of abandonment or rejection

★   extreme high and low mood swings

★   low self-esteem and self-worth

★   lots of partners, breakups, and new "loves"

★   openly seductive or manipulative behavior to get what she wants

★   drug or alcohol abuse

What Action to Take

★   Talk openly about your concerns for your daughter's physical and emotional well-being.

★   Explain what you know about why girl's become sexually promiscuous.

★   Assure her that with professional help, she can learn to meet her needs without sacrificing herself in the process.

★   Discuss health risks and give her written information on them.

★   Schedule a medical checkup immediately and encourage her to be open with the doctor about all the activities she has participated in.

★   Find a counselor or therapist with whom your daughter feels comfortable and seek ongoing treatment as soon as possible.

★   Be willing and open to family counseling if recommended.

★ Look for ways to build up her self-esteem and self-worth.

★ Reassure her that you love her unconditionally and will support her in any way you can.

Feeling Emotionally Troubled about Sex

Some adolescent girls struggle with feelings of extreme guilt or fears around their emerging sexuality. A seventeen-year-old girl described the following situation to me before being allowed to permanently leave her parents and live with a family that was granted legal custody of her:

> I think something's wrong with me. I don't think about sex or ever want it when I'm with my boyfriend. It repulses me and makes me feel dirty to even think about it. Maybe it's because of my dad. He has teased me about my breast size for a long time. He jokes about how "hot" I look. He struts around the house holding up my new bras and underwear, saying how "sexy" my "jugs" are. He does that in front of my brothers and sister and mom. He even did it one night when family friends came over. It's so embarrassing and humiliating. Why does he care? Everyone laughs. It's a big joke. Now my brothers do it, too. Even my mom laughs along. When I try to tell my mom it's wrong and inappropriate for him to do that to me, she tells me to "take a joke." She thinks I overreact for nothing and then gets mad at me for getting upset about it. Am I right to feel this is very wrong for him to do to me?

Look and Listen for These Signs

★ exposure to a sexually traumatic experience

★ exposure to pornography and other forms of media that depict sexual trauma or confusing messages about women

★ spiritual and religious conflicts about choices and behaviors

★ a negative attitude toward her body or sexuality in general

★ fears of infection, inadequacy, and disapproval

★ fears and/or avoidance of intimacy and dating

What Action to Take

✶ Explain your concerns.

✶ Reassure your daughter that if she is struggling with such emotions that she is responding the way she is for a good reason.

✶ Assure her that she can learn to view sexuality in a healthy and comfortable way with the help of a professional. Find a counselor or therapist whom your daughter can trust.

✶ Support her need for confidentiality and privacy. (In other words, assure her you won't pry or insist on knowing what her counseling sessions are about.)

✶ Assure her that with time she can experience a sexually satisfying relationship when she's ready.

✶ Set a positive example by exhibiting a healthy attitude and approach toward sexuality.

✶ Discuss how you think about and respond to unhealthy sexual messages in our culture.

STRETCHING EXERCISES

Use the following exercises to encourage discussion, understanding, and responsible decision-making around the sexual issues your daughter will face as a teen.

Exercise: Sex 101

You might try asking your daughter the following questions to stimulate discussion:

✶ "Who of your friends do you think knows the most about sex? Why?"

✶ "Who of your friends do you imagine knows the least about sex? Why?"

✶ "Who do you imagine explained sex to me?" (Talk to her about how you first learned about sex. Girls generally like to hear your stories more than they like to focus on themselves. Talk with your daughter about who and what your best and worst sources of information about sexuality were.)

★   "I read or heard about a bumper sticker that said something like, 'Put on a condom once or put on diapers for years.' Do you think that's a good message? Why or why not?"

Exercise: Take a Research Trip

★   Ask your gynecologist or family-planning clinic for written information you can share with your daughter.

★   Visit a library or bookstore and review books about teen sexuality or general sex education that might be helpful to share with your daughter. Give your daughter the books you want her to read. (Girls have told me they read every word and study every picture when they have complete privacy.) Casually follow up with your daughter about it after some time has passed.

Here are a few examples of what you might ask: Did you think the book about sex I gave you was well written? Was it too young or too old for you? Was it easy to understand or confusing? Is there anything in there so far that you have questions about? Do you think the book really understands what girls want to know and need to know? Talk to her about what you like about the book, and discuss any important issues that you think the book leaves out.

Exercise: Raise a Critical Thinker

Pay attention to cultural messages about sex and learn to directly expose them wherever you see them. Encourage awareness, self-reflection, and discussion by asking your daughter the following questions:

★   "What does this message imply or teach?"

★   "Who does this message hurt, and why?"

★   "What is the truth in the message? What is the lie?""

★ "What stereotypes do you see? What do they lead you to believe?"

★ "What positive messages do you see about sex? How are they different?"

Exercise: Write a "Sexual Code of Conduct"

Challenge your daughter to write her own personal and confidential sexual code of conduct based on her values and beliefs. You might suggest including statements about:

★ her commitment to herself, partner, and beliefs

★ her expectations of how she should be treated

★ how her body will be honored

★ what her values and beliefs are about sexual relationships

★ what decisions she has made about *what she will do, when she will do it,* and *with whom* she will share a sexual relationship

★ safety measures she will remember to practice

CHAPTER 6

Promoting a Healthy Lifestyle

I hate looking in my mirror. I look fat. I wish I could do something about it. If a chick is fat, she's a total loser. I've been thinking about trying to work out and tone up. I feel so much better when I'm active, but I have no time to do sports. I've got to do something! I hate my body! I'm so embarrassed. I feel like such a blob. Help!

—Diary entry from a sixteen-year-old girl

For the most part, adolescence is a healthy time of life. Teenage girls are on the go and involved in a variety of activities that contribute to their health and well-being. But few teenage girls are satisfied with their appearance. Negative self-appraisal seems to attack a girl's self-esteem more than negative experiences in sports, school, and friendships. Helping your daughter cultivate a healthy lifestyle can influence the way she perceives herself. Establishing a way of life that promotes an overall sense of well-being directly impacts her self-esteem.

Nutrition, exercise, sleep, and recreation are all important aspects of your daughter's health, contributing to her appearance and good physical and mental functioning. If she's like most teens, she probably pays the most attention to recreational activities. Nutrition, exercise, and sleep may be another story.

At this age, your daughter is probably growing less and less interested in what you have to say about the ways she should be taking care of herself. She may not appreciate or even pay attention when you point out the consequences of "unhealthy habits." Most moms say they watch their daughters roll their eyes when they offer a helpful suggestion or two. For many girls, motherly advice is now annoying advice that they don't want to listen to.

If your daughter can't get to sleep before ten at night, gags at the thought of drinking milk, and hates exercise or competitive sports, you may have a typical teen on your hands. Some girls enjoy drinking espressos, like to smoke cigarettes, and are determined not to go off their steady diet of junk foods. Throw in a little alcohol and drugs and it's a mother's nightmare.

Mothers invariably ponder the ways they can impress upon their girls the importance of living a healthy lifestyle. Just because your daughter tunes you out doesn't mean you should give up and stop trying to influence her habits. You may just need to go about it in a different way.

A BALANCE OF ACTIVITIES

It's important for your daughter to find a healthy balance in the activities and behaviors that affect her health. It may be challenging for her to spend enough time in all the areas important to her development if she is overextended or experiencing pressure from any number of sources. Juggling sleep, meals, social events, and school and work schedules can be tough even for the most organized girl. However, your daughter needs ample time to take care of herself. Getting enough rest, eating right, and engaging in daily doses of play and exercise will strengthen her physical, mental, and emotional resiliency.

It's normal to care about your daughter's health and to be concerned about it, but it's important to empower *her* to make the changes she needs to make in order to find balance. Rather than focus on what she may not be doing right, spend your time directly noticing the consequences of the choices she's made. There are approaches you can take that will help your daughter consider more carefully the decisions she makes around sleep, nutrition, and physical activity.

I Need My Beauty Sleep

Somewhere in the world, on any given weekend, there's a teenager complaining about having to get out of bed before lunchtime. When I try to rouse the fourteen-year-old I know best out of a comatose state of slumber, I hear this: "I need my beauty sleep, leave me alone!" She readjusts her pink satin eye mask with the word "princess" embroidered on the front and "goes under" again.

Sleeping until noon may seem to make no sense, especially if you enjoy being an early riser. But when your daughter says she needs sleep, she's right. She needs a lot of it.

At this age, most adolescents are likely to experience different patterns in their sleep cycles. Your daughter may feel her best when she has stayed up late at night and slept longer in the morning. When she is sleep deprived, she is likely to achieve less in school, and suffer from depression more often. Some high schools have wisely adjusted their schedules to accommodate this physiological change. To help students perform more successfully in school, they have decided to start and end the school day later.

Getting the right amount of sleep will contribute to your daughter's overall beauty and happiness. You can encourage her to establish a sleep schedule that works for her.

What You Can Say

Instead of: You stayed up too late and now you're paying for it. I tell you over and over again to get to bed on time!

Try: Yup, that's how it feels when you don't give yourself enough hours to sleep. Everything is harder when you're tired. It's difficult to feel and look your best when you feel so worn out.

Instead of: Get to bed! You need your sleep!

Try: How many hours of sleep do you find you need to really feel your best? How many hours of sleep are you going to give yourself tonight?

There's Nothing to Eat

Most adolescents have terrible diets during the teen years. They are prone to fad diets, eating on the run, and consuming a lot of empty calories. Soda, chips, french fries, and candy are not the four basic food groups recommended, but they are nevertheless the ones teens typically consume. The mother of two teenage daughters told me this:

> I pride myself in keeping healthy snacks out and always within reach of my kids. Our kitchen shelves are amply stocked and my husband or I prepare a full dinner almost every night. Even with a table full of food in front of them I hear daily, "There's nothing to eat!" What they really mean is, if it's not fast food, they aren't interested.

One mother said she set up a consultation for her daughter with a "hip, young dietitian she could relate to." Her daughter was eating so poorly and feeling so unhappy about her weight that she knew some education from a neutral person might be helpful. She said this:

> My daughter barely gave me the time of day when it came to discussing her diet. But she was completely open to listening and learning from the dietitian. She was an "authority" and knew better than me. So my daughter took her advice to heart and improved her nutrition in ways I would never have thought possible. I think learning what she did even helped prevent some unhealthy habits from forming that could have put her at risk for an eating disorder.

A mother who pressures her daughter to lose weight, watch the scale, or focus a great deal of attention on food intake is more likely to encourage poor habits than to help her daughter overcome them. Not only will her daughter be more likely to gain weight, but she may suffer emotional abandonment for never feeling accepted for who she is. Serious eating disorders are sometimes the result. (See the Warning Signs at the end of this chapter for more information on eating disorders).

Your daughter needs nutritional information and encouragement for trying new foods outside the junk food chain. Help her explore alternatives and options that will benefit her diet.

What You Can Say

Instead of:　You have to drink milk! Your bones and teeth can't grow without it. You have to have calcium or you're putting yourself at risk for all kinds of problems.

Try:　You're old enough now to take responsibility for your health. I know you hate milk, so why don't you take a look at some of the calcium supplements available and pick one out. That way you'll be getting what you need and it'll be easier to take.

Instead of: Why didn't you eat more for lunch? You're always complaining you're hungry and I keep telling you that it's important to eat more protein. You need more than sugar to fill you up!

Try: Candy bars don't always fill you up for long. I hate being hungry when I'm working. Sounds like you need to try making some different choices and work some protein into your diet.

Instead of: You're addicted to cigarettes and espressos. When are you going to quit? You're giving yourself cancer! Why can't you drink something good for you in the morning?

Try: You've made the choice to practice habits that are really tough to stop. Addictive behaviors sneak up on teens as easily as they do adults. Have you thought about quitting? When you're ready, I'll help you come up with a plan. I care about the short-term and long-term consequences for your health.

I Don't Have Time to Become an Olympic Athlete

Some girls say they have been "turned off" to exercise or feel resentful because parents pressure them to participate in activities they don't really enjoy. Others say the financial burdens and time commitments make it hard for their families to support their participation. Some express feelings of awkwardness and self-consciousness because they see themselves as "nonathletic." And other girls say playing sports is their life.

Overactivity or underactivity are both unhealthy extremes that can influence your daughter's physical fitness. A comfortable balance of physical activities can give your daughter a powerful sense of accomplishment and excitement. It's important to provide opportunities for girls to participate in something that interests them. Even when sports or exercise isn't the focus of their lives, most girls who stay open to trying new activities eventually find something they can feel passionate about doing. Many women have experienced lifelong benefits from physical activities they learned as teens.

Sometimes, however, parents put such an emphasis on their daughters' sports lives that "playing" becomes a chore and girls may be less invested. It can also be difficult to inspire girls who have never had the desire to be physically active. The mother of a fourteen-year-old girl shared this experience:

No matter how much I have pressured or encouraged her to get involved in some sort of physical activity, she always has an excuse to stay in front of the computer or behind a book. The other day I asked her to join me for a walk. She snapped, "I don't have enough time to become an Olympic athlete, okay?" I told her I didn't realize they gave gold medals for walking dogs!

You can't always be the one to motivate your daughter. She will benefit from learning how to motivate herself. However, you may be able to inspire her to think and feel differently when you pressure her less and encourage her more.

What You Can Say

Instead of: You can't make friends and stay in shape if you don't play sports and stay active this year. You need to sign up and commit to something.

Try: What sport do you enjoy the most? The least? What do you feel you can make a commitment to doing on a regular basis? What will you try this year?

Instead of: You say you don't want to be fat, but you aren't doing what you need to do! I keep telling you that you need to get out and exercise, so you can get your weight down, but you won't listen. To lose fat, you have to exercise and cut your calories at the same time. You've got to keep up your heart rate to burn enough calories. You're going to keep gaining if you don't listen to me!

Try: Let me know how I can help. I can see this is important to you and I think it's great that you care about taking care of your physical health. Eating healthier foods and exercising helps all of us feel and look better. I admire your motivation. We all feel happier when we feel good about our bodies.

LETTING GO OF HER RESPONSIBILITY

Balancing your expectations of your daughter can be just as important as helping her learn to balance her life with healthy activities and behaviors. If you feel completely responsible for your daughter's health choices, it may be time to shift the responsibility back to her.

It's normal for moms to feel troubled by a daughter's feelings of fatigue due to lack of sleep, to feel concerned about irritability and lack of energy from consuming a poor diet, or to worry about the health risks of obesity, lack of exercise, caffeine consumption, and tobacco use. But it's also important to learn to let go of your feelings of responsibility for her lifestyle choices.

Just as the alcoholic can only stop drinking when she does it for herself, not to please others, your daughter must act on her own behalf, not yours. Instilling self-motivation is easier when you let go and give your daughter the reins. She needs to find within herself the reason for her goals and actions. She needs to make changes on her own terms, not yours. It doesn't usually work any other way.

MONSTER IN THE MIRROR

Body image is a powerful issue for many women. If girls develop a positive attitude and concept of their appearance when they're still young, they often enter into adulthood with greater confidence and self-esteem.

Teens can spend hours in front of mirrors worrying about their skin, hair, face, weight, and clothes. Girls of all shapes, sizes, and athletic ability typically say there's something about themselves they wish they could change. Real or perceived, most girls don't escape adolescence without some amount of discomfort about their physical appearance.

Your daughter's self-evaluation is likely to be very different from the opinions of others. Especially yours. A fourteen-year-old girl said: "Of course my mom is going to say I'm beautiful and perfect, because she's my mom! She doesn't count."

Saying nothing to your daughter about her special qualities is worse than having your comments discounted. It's important to share freely and honestly on a consistent basis what you love about your daughter, including her appearance and strengths as a person. She may not respond or agree with your assessments, but she hears them. A fifteen-year-old girl told me: "I know my mom is biased, being my mom and all, but I can trust her to be honest with me. I ask her opinions about my hair, makeup, and clothes. I'm glad she tells me what she thinks. She doesn't know it, but sometimes the compliments she gives me help when I'm feeling down on myself."

Reactions of other people can leave lasting impressions, and sometimes comments can be so hurtful that teens remember them for life. Jeanette, a seventeen-year-old, shared the following experience that she says has continued to haunt her throughout her teen years:

I was almost eleven when we had a big family get-together at our house. My sisters and cousins and I were all lined up in the kitchen waiting for lunch. One of our relatives commented on how fast we were all growing up. One by one, she commented on the changes in each of us, talking about things like our height, legs, figure, or complexion, or something nice. When she got to me she paused and said, "Well, Jeanette still has her baby fat, she's still pretty plump, but hopefully she still has time to outgrow that." Up to that moment, I never realized I looked fat to others. From then on, I felt different and bigger and self-conscious around everyone. I was so shocked and repulsed by myself that I forgot about my hunger and went into my room and hid in the closet. I was stunned by what she had said. I never wanted to be seen again! I hated myself, partly because I was "fat" and partly because I couldn't love myself anymore, the way I used to. Until that moment I had liked and appreciated my freckles, scars, and all. When my mother found me hiding, she opened the closet door and told me to just ignore what she had said. But I never forgot it. Not ever.

Most girls say they want to be thinner. At a time when obesity is on the rise in our country, adolescent girls may be hearing the message that losing weight and fighting fat is the thing to do. Many teen girls say that they start smoking because it helps them keep their weight down and they fear they'll "get fat" if they quit. Girls hear from the culture that women should be thin and shapely. However, the majority of adolescent girls are not fashion models, sports heroes, or movie stars. A fourteen-year-old girl told me: "We compare ourselves to magazine models, even though I know we aren't supposed to. But I always say to myself things like, 'I wish my butt wasn't as big. I wish it were just like hers in the magazine!' I feel like I need to be perfect to be happy. That scares me because I know that's how eating disorders get started. I've seen it happen to my friends." And a sixteen–year-old girl said: "Of course we're obsessed with our weight! The fatter you are, the less dates and boyfriends you get. Maybe it shouldn't be that way, but that's the way it is."

A Distorted View

It's normal for your daughter to spend an inordinate amount of time in front of a mirror waiting perhaps for the signs of an emerging look she can relax with. But when a girl sees something negative in her reflection, she can also develop a distorted view of her appearance. A negative body image can have a profound effect on a girl's feelings about herself and her level of confidence. The following is from a poem written by a fifteen-year-old girl:

> *When she looks in the mirror*
> *What does she see?*
> *She sees fat, feels ugly and zitty,*
> *But when others look at her, they think she's pretty . . .*
> *This is something every girl knows,*
> *Whether it happens to her or another . . .*
> *A monster can emerge in the mirror . . .*
> *If only someone could tell her the monster isn't her that appears.*

You can help your daughter develop a positive body image that will boost her self-esteem, social acceptance, and an overall satisfaction about life. Remember, understanding can have far-reaching benefits.

What You Can Do

★ Be aware of the influence social pressures have on girls' perceptions of their appearance.

★ Help your daughter resist societal pressure to conform to unrealistic standards. Don't attach great importance to weight, physical appearance, and attractiveness.

★ Offer guidance on healthy nutrition.

★ Explain the process of developing a body image. Talk to her about the risk of developing a distorted self-image.

★ Talk to your daughter about the appreciation women can have for their bodies when they see them as a sacred part of themselves.

★ Keep your expectations realistic for her achievement and social acceptance.

★ Don't overprotect. Give her autonomy.

★ Avoid controlling too many things. You need to recognize your daughter as an individual in her own right, separate from you.

★ To boost her self-confidence, let her make her own decisions.

★ Don't belittle her self-preoccupation, but remember it's normal and to be expected.

★ Provide your daughter with practical help when possible. For example, allow her to pick out new clothes, encourage her to exercise with you, offer medical treatment if needed for acne, agree to help her improve her smile and teeth, help her find a hairstyle and "look" that she feels good in.

The mother of a thirteen-year-old girl helped her daughter this way:

My daughter's friends have all developed already. This is a big issue for her because she has no breasts at all yet. Everyone has boobs but her, and she keeps asking me, "What's wrong with me, Mom?" I've tried all the normal answers—told her to be patient, that it's what's on the inside that counts, and all that—but you know what? What helped her the most was when I offered to buy her a padded bra. I explained that she looked beautiful to me already, but that if it would help her feel more confident, I would be willing to spring for it. She was thrilled! I saw all her spark and confidence come back! Sometimes it can be important to help nature out a little during these vulnerable years.

EVERYONE ELSE WAS DOING IT: DRUGS, ALCOHOL, AND PEER PRESSURE

Drinking, smoking, inhaling, snorting, shooting up: some teens go to great lengths to get high. Your daughter is not immune from the danger. Chances are she will be faced with choices to experiment with illegal substances. It's difficult, if not impossible, for teens to completely escape the culture of drugs they live in. In the United States, drug use is pervasive. According to the U.S. Department of Health and Human Services (1999), by the age of fourteen, 81 percent of all teens have tried drinking, 56 percent have tried smoking cigarettes, and 39 percent have tried an illegal drug (usually marijuana). Mothers have reason to be frightened.

By the time girls reach adolescence, they are growing intensely curious about "adult-like" behaviors. Even great students who get along well with their parents, and are psychologically healthy, sociable, and well liked by their peers are not immune to the influences of peer pressure or their own natural curiosity.

In many cases, girls are behaving in the same ways they see adults, parents, older siblings, and peers behave. There is widespread use and availability of substances almost anywhere you live.

Our society seems to be growing increasingly drug dependent. Girls can watch as adults and friends routinely use caffeine to wake up, cigarettes to calm down, a drink before dinner to cope with stress, and other antidotes to relieve anxiety or depression.

Still, when girls have been educated all their lives about the dangers of alcohol, tobacco, and illicit drugs and seem to have no apparent reason for escape, mothers struggle with "why" or "how" their daughters could be so easily influenced into trying something so dangerous to their health.

Straight Talk from Moms

★ *This is not my favorite time. The teen years are my least preferred as a mother because of the all the stuff they come into contact with.*

★ *The use of drugs and alcohol is accepted behavior among teens. Too many kids don't have any reasons not to engage in these behaviors.*

★ *I tell my daughter that it's not a question of "if" it will happen around you, it's a question of "when." They have to be prepared and think ahead.*

★ *As a mom, I want to give my daughters some backbone. I want them to be able to stand up and do what's right. Too many teens just don't care. The acceptance they want from others and the need to cut loose and feel some freedom may override everything they've learned.*

★ *If you have a mad crush on the guy who's rolling the joint, your desire to impress him might be greater than personal values and beliefs about drugs. We need to help our girls care more about themselves than about pleasing others. How do we strengthen them enough to be able to resist peer pressure?*

The Power of Resistance

As mothers, sometimes we control too much and forget to let our daughters practice taking their own control. The power to resist peer pressure and other temptations grows from a girl's ability to make her own choices and day-to-day decisions about her life.

Even minor choices, such as what classes your daughter will enroll in, clothes she will wear, sports teams she will join, clubs she will participate in, hairstyles she will try, or parties she will plan, give her valuable practice in identifying her wants and needs. She also gains the satisfaction of knowing how she can take responsibility for her own happiness. The mother of a fifteen-year-old girl said this:

> As hard as it can be to let go, we have to give our daughter enough "safe" freedoms and choices in her day-to-day life and activities, to help her develop confidence in making decisions for herself. How well she resists peer pressure has a lot to do with how much practice we've given her in defining who she is and what she wants to do. If a mom is controlling everything about her daughter's life, she may be prohibiting her from learning to be her own person.

When girls aren't allowed to direct their own destiny, they miss out on opportunities that build up their strength and self-confidence. If your daughter is expected to please you and conform to your choices, she may never learn how to resist conforming to others.

When girls grow up with the message that they must please others and always put their wishes and desires behind those of others, they may be more vulnerable to group conformity and peer pressure. Many have not learned that it's possible to think and act separately and independently for themselves.

The gratification that comes from belonging, being popular, and "fitting in with the crowd" is difficult for a lot of girls to resist. When everyone else is experimenting with drugs and alcohol, suddenly there may be no good reason not to join in. Your daughter needs to know how to develop confidence in saying "no." It's important to help her internalize a positive attitude toward peer pressure and a sense of self-confidence when she is confronted by it.

What You Can Tell Her

★ "Before you try something new, stop and listen to your feelings."

★ "There's a healthy and unhealthy way to do almost everything in life. Sex, music, dress, eating, fun, recreation, alcohol, drugs. It's how you choose to behave in these areas that can be problematic, not the activities themselves. Ask yourself if this is a choice that is clearly a healthy one."

★ "Fear is a helpful emotion. It can signal when you are in a situation that you need to get out of. Use your instinctual sense of fear to help you stay out of trouble."

- ★ "Remember, you are especially vulnerable when you have a question or doubt about what you should do. That's an important indication that you're stepping into something that you might regret."

- ★ "Decide what you want to be known for."

- ★ "Make a commitment to your own health and safety."

- ★ "Friends who want you to join them in illegal or dangerous activity don't really care about you. It's okay not to be liked by people who don't have your best interest at heart."

- ★ "It's okay to be different from others in your group."

- ★ "If you set your mind to it, you can say 'no.'"

- ★ "Practice one phrase you will use whenever confronted to make a potentially dangerous choice. For example: 'No thanks. I don't use.'"

- ★ "Establish clear goals for what you will and will not do in your life."

- ★ "Think about what using drugs or alcohol might do for you, that you can't do for yourself in any other way."

Inform and Educate

It's important to directly explain the risks of using alcohol and other drugs to your daughter, but try not to use scare tactics. If she believes you are exaggerating the risks, she may not believe there's any danger at all.

What You Can Do

- ★ Be informed about the hazards and share them openly and directly. Your silence about the use of substances may imply consent.

- ★ Educate her regarding the dangers.

- ★ Teach skills that resist peer pressure.

- ★ Teach strategies for handling life stress.

- ★ Model the right behavior. In other words, do what you say. Parental substance abuse is a powerful influence on your daughter's choice to use.

★ Confront the facts. Using substances helps some girls temporarily and artificially overcome shyness and a sense of awkwardness. Drugs may provide a means to find relief, comfort, confidence, and security. Some teens use it to enhance sexual pleasure, decrease tension, or increase their sense of belonging.

★ Don't forget to communicate the hard lessons you have learned through your own experiences or through the experiences of others close to you.

★ Consistently monitor your daughter's activities and friends.

★ Know where your daughter goes for fun and what supervision is provided.

★ Help her learn to express herself clearly, directly, and confidently.

★ To boost her self-confidence, let your daughter make her own decisions .

★ It's dangerous to take any "experimentation" lightly that your daughter may have engaged in. Plan ahead how you will respond if it happens and be clear about the consequences. (For example, you will take away her driving privileges.)

What You Can Say

★ "Using drugs or alcohol never eases emotional problems; it makes them worse over time."

★ "Among other risks, pot can affect motivation and impair your judgment and acquisition of knowledge."

★ "Before making an important decision, think about the consequences."

★ "Smoking regularly when young can reduce your sexual and reproductive maturation process."

★ "Using or carrying illegal substances is against the law and can earn you a criminal record."

★ "Trying a mood-altering substance even once can dangerously impair your perception, thinking, and judgment. Drug abuse can lead to permanent injury or death."

★ "Drinking alcohol at parties and from open containers may be dangerous, since drinks can be easily spiked with such drugs as the 'rape drug' designed to immobilize you."

★ "It only takes one time to suffer severe consequences."

A HEALTHY HEART AND SOUL

Language has the power to nourish or infect. Radiant beauty springs from a healthy, well-nourished heart and soul. Many mothers believe that when teens are exposed to a constant onslaught of derogatory language, the damage can be toxic.

Without listing all the profanities that can be heard on any given day in the corridors of homes, schools, or any public site, it's probably safe to say that sex, religion, ethnicity, and homosexuality continue to inspire enough discomfort in people to illicit the "bad" or "dirty" words used in our culture. Most girls never think of toxic language as being hate words directed against certain groups, but then neither do most adults. Words of hate and violence are also targeted at women on a regular basis. Some of the words do hurt and confuse young girls. They sense the disrespect. A sixteen-year-old girl told me: "I walked by this group of older guys who started calling me names with whistles and smacking noises. I didn't even know what some of the words meant; I just knew how it felt. I couldn't get away fast enough. I felt totally naked. Like they saw the most personal and private parts of me without my permission. They invaded my privacy."

Words of hate and violence often target women in the media. Many moms believe that angry and destructive forms of communication are like pollution to the ears. One mother put it this way: "'Word pollution' is everywhere. Our teens are learning to use toxic language as easily as they use the drinking fountain. When our girls listen to this day in and day out, in all areas of our culture, it has to impact emotional and spiritual health. Especially when much of it is created to describe women in a degrading way."

Straight Talk from Daughters

★ *That's the language we use today. Parents are too old-fashioned.*

★ *It doesn't mean anything. That's just the way everyone talks.*

★ *We don't listen to the words or lyrics, we just like the music.*

★ *All the songs sing about something or have something in them that my mom isn't going to like, so what can you do?*

★ *What's the big f------ deal? That's why we talk this way, I don't care who I shock. They're only words. I mean, come on! It's not my problem if my parents can't handle it.*

★ *I learned my worst words from my mom and dad. They don't care when they use bad language. Why should I get grounded when I do? Talk about hypocrites!*

★ *Everyone talks that way. Even when guys call a girl a bitch, it's just a joke. We're used to it. I mean it's actually kind of funny."*

★ *I think people talk that way to sound cool. It's the only way they can sound tough and get attention.*

★ *I get in the habit of cussing because all my friends do, and I'm around them all day. Sometimes I slip at home and my mom is like, "What did you say?" and I have to hurry and cover it up. It's totally a habit with me, but I do want to stop it because I don't want to sound cheap.*

★ *I don't feel good about myself when I use bad language. There's always another way I could've expressed myself. It's just easier to use it sometimes.*

★ *It's just a way to be entertaining and dramatic, you know, like in the movies.*

★ *I think it's actually embarrassing that in the movies writers can't create any better lines than they do. Like, maybe they could expand their vocabulary a little from just dirty words?*

★ *I don't worry about it. I don't even think about it. It doesn't offend me. People should be free to talk any way they want.*

A Breath of Fresh Air

The mother of three teenage girls has a "clean air act" in effect in her home and car. She says this:

Even if girls have only one place where they have to stop and think about the way their words affect people or what they mean, it's valuable. I want my daughters and their friends to think before they act or speak. Then decide if it's what they really want or meant to say. They have discussions around how others perceive their words. It becomes a peer discussion rather than me lecturing. They may not realize how degrading their language is to all women. On some level that hurts them. I'm inclined to believe it hurts all girls. It certainly can't do anything for them.

The daughters of this mom told me the "clean air act" she enforces generates a lot of lively conversation about the meanings of words. Some girls have been shocked to find out what certain words have been derived from. It makes them think twice.

WARNING SIGNS

There are serious health hazards that mothers may have to contend with. Eating disorders and substance abuse are two important issues that impact a number of teenage girls. You can watch for certain warning signs listed below, but keep in mind that every situation is different.

Eating Disorders

Nutrition can be adversely affected by a preoccupation with being thin. It is not uncommon for these preoccupations to quickly or gradually become life-threatening situations. Eating disorders such as *anorexia nervosa* or *bulimia* may result in damage to vital organs, kidney failure, permanent loss of bone mass, brain damage, and death.

When girls no longer enjoy eating, and have an intense fear of gaining weight, their obsessions about food can result in an eating disorder. For these girls, food becomes an enemy that must be battled. A thirteen-year-old girl shared the following: "Me. I'm just your average teenager. I get good grades, have lots of friends, play sports, and am the queen of my school. Like, I'm the most popular. And that's really fun. I think I'm anorexic, though. I've lost thirty pounds from my old weight of 110. And god, am I glad, because I looked like a pig back then. I do look kind of pale, but oh, well. I mean, at least I'm losing weight, right?"

Signs of Anorexia

★ distorted body image

★ compulsive fear of getting fat

★ avoidance of food when hungry

★ self-starvation

★ compulsive dieting

★ wearing baggy clothes to hide thinness or complaining that regular clothes are too tight

★ becoming increasingly withdrawn, secretive, and isolated from others

★ compulsive exercising

★ menstrual periods that don't start or stop

★ pale skin and brittle, discolored nails

★ fine dark hair over her body

★ extreme sensitivity to cold

★ perfectionist behavior; setting inordinately high standards for self

★ denial of any problem, resistance to treatment

What Action to Take

★ Set up an appointment for a medical evaluation with your daughter's physician as soon as possible. Early detection is important.

★ Consult with an eating disorders specialist.

★ Hospitalization may be necessary; a combination of individual and family therapy is usually recommended.

★ Encourage your daughter's involvement in support groups and educational groups regarding nutrition.

★ Expect treatment to move slowly. Her behaviors aren't likely to change quickly.

Signs of Bulimia

★ binge and purge cycles (consuming a large amount of food in a short period of time and then purging it, through self-induced vomiting or the use of laxatives)

★ fluctuating weight

★ fear of getting fat

★ irregular menstrual periods

★ tooth decay

★ puffy face and throat

★ dizziness or blackouts

★ dehydration, upset stomach, constipation, sore throat

★ secretiveness about food

★ stealing or hoarding food in strange places

★ lonely, unhappy, anxious behavior

★ depression

★ substance abuse

★ childhood physical or sexual trauma

★ family with high expectations

Take the same actions you would take if your daughter were anorexic. Unlike anorexics, however, girls with bulimia often have an awareness of their eating disorder and may be more receptive to treatment.

Substance Abuse

Experimentation with drugs does not always lead to abuse and addiction. But when it does, it almost certainly upsets a teen's physical and psychological development. Most adolescents who move from experimentation to abuse or addiction are seriously troubled. Many have failed to learn responsible decision-making skills and alternative coping techniques for their problems.

Signs of Drug Abuse

★ friends and peers who encourage risk-taking and use of substances

★ friends who have access to substances

★ impulsive, disruptive behaviors

★ moodiness, anxiety, depression

★ sudden drop in grades

★ secretive, uncommunicative behavior

★ confused, disoriented, lethargic behavior

★ dishonesty, lying, stealing

★ defensiveness

★ money or items missing from home

★ not following through with responsibilities

★ skipping classes, tardiness, incompletes

★ changes in sleeping, eating habits, or hygiene

★ bloodshot or glassy eyes, dull skin color, odor

What Action to Take

★ Don't ignore the problem. Confront your daughter with facts about her behavior.

★ Stay calm and express a willingness to help.

★ Seek help and consultation from a substance abuse treatment specialist. Contact a drug hotline, mental health center, school counselor, or your health-care provider for advice. Hospitalization or admitting your daughter into a treatment program may be the necessary first step.

★ Be patient with treatment. Relapse rates are high. It's not uncommon for teens to need to repeat treatment.

STRETCHING EXERCISES

Try the following exercises to help promote a healthy lifestyle for your daughter and to help prevent her from making unhealthy choices.

Exercise: Balancing the Wheel of Life

To help increase your daughter's awareness of how balanced her life activities are, try the following technique. Draw a large circle on a piece of paper. Make a list of the following categories (feel free to make any additions or changes to this list):

1. time for physical activity

2. time for nutritious meals

3. time for sleep

4. time for play (including friends)

5. time for work (if she has a job)

6. time for school

7. time for family

8. time for privacy

9. time for spiritual growth

10. miscellaneous (community service, clubs, etc.)

Ask your daughter to cut up the wheel into ten slices according to the amount of time and attention she is able to give each category. Ask her: What parts are too big or too small? Where is the wheel out of balance? What can she do to bring the wheel into better balance? Explain that when wheels are out of balance, nothing runs smoothly and they are less efficient. When balanced, your life can run more smoothly.

Exercise: What I Wouldn't Change List

Ask your daughter to think about what she loves about herself. Have her list *at least one* quality she would never want to change in each of the following categories:

★ personality strengths (how I act):

★ talents/abilities (what I can do):

★ physical appearance (how I look):

★ beliefs/values (who I am):

Make your own list of what you observe in your daughter and ask her best friend to come up with another list. Encourage your daughter to post all three lists on her mirror.

Exercise: Personal Choice Inventory

Take a look at the ways you currently help your daughter practice personal choices and decision-making. Ask your daughter to answer the following questions by making a list for each answer:

1. What choices do I make on a regular basis that impact my life?

2. What choices would I like to have more freedom making?

Ask yourself if your daughter has enough practice in controlling her own destiny. Are there more decisions you can give her responsibility for making that will ultimately increase her sense of confidence and strengthen her ability to resist peer pressure?

Exercise: Pressure Response

Encourage your daughter to write a sentence or phrase and remember it when tempted by peer pressure. *This is the statement or phrase I will carry in my mind and use when asked to do something I know (or believe) is a negative choice for myself:* _____

CHAPTER 7

Forming Positive Relationships

Here I am, sitting in my room listening to such a depressing song. It reminds me of Ryan. Everything reminds me of Ryan. I can't get him out of my head. Before he moved, we hung out as much as possible. We flirted, but nothing ever happened. He never said anything, but neither did I. I never realized how much I liked him until it was too late. He's even in my dreams. If I could go back I would tell him how I feel. But now it's too late. And the thing that really gets me is I'll never see him again . . . I wonder if he ever thinks of me.

—Diary entry from a fourteen-year-old girl

Teenage girls may agonize about relationships that never sparked into more than a friendship. They may spend hours or even days ruminating about "what might have been." In hindsight they may believe they missed the chance to experience a romance of epic proportions and feel tortured by the idea that they may have lost the "love of their life." But the despair experienced in such situations can hold a sense of excitement and romanticism, too. Teenage girls suddenly realize they feel more like women than girls.

Even when relationships are never fully actualized, they remain vital to your daughter's development. Many experiences provide important opportunities for self-discovery. As her life broadens and expands, your daughter will be exposed to more adults and authority figures. However, they are unlikely to be the major focus of her attention. Friends and romantic interests usually mean a whole lot more.

Romantic attractions and an increasing desire for relationships with peers provide special emotional fulfillment, as your daughter grows more emotionally independent from you. Your daughter needs the companionship of her peers on her journey to womanhood.

HER RELATIONSHIP CHOICES

Your daughter may be able to create and solve complex problems with brilliant logic, but she may not always be as reasonable, mature, or consistent in her thinking when it comes to people and social relationships. You may wholeheartedly approve of some of your daughter's affiliations, but question others. There may be times when you instinctively feel alarmed or uncertain about someone she is associating with. You may be afraid that negative choices may limit or alter the direction of her life. Most mothers hope the relationships their daughters enter into will enhance their lives, not complicate them more.

Most girls tend to select friends who reflect the image they have of themselves. Girls who feel insecure may be attracted to insecure friends. Others may select friends as a way to rebel against their parent(s). The mother of a sixteen-year-old girl shared this story:

> I took my daughter to school one morning and we argued and bickered the whole drive in. It was just one of those "off" days when I felt like everything was wrong between us. She slammed the door when she got out of the car and never looked back. I sat there for a while feeling sorry for myself, wondering how things could possibly get any worse between us. And then I saw this guy walk by wearing a beat-up black leather jacket with baggy pants hanging so low they exposed the crack in his rear. His hair was greasy and fell over his eyes. I could hear the chains swinging on one of his hips as he sauntered past my car, and I counted eight pierced earrings on his face. I thought to myself, "Okay! Things *could* be worse! At least my daughter isn't dating *him*." I drove away in a happier mood and realized it was important to get things in perspective sometimes.

The next night my daughter brought her new boyfriend home for dinner. *He* walked in. I must have turned white because my husband said I looked like I had seen a ghost. At that moment I wished I had. Then maybe he could've disappeared! But there he was, as real as could be, still adorned by the same leather jacket, baggy pants, chains, earrings, and greasy hair. Things really were worse after all.

I'm ashamed to admit that I sat through dinner hoping he'd choke on his steak and have to leave early. It didn't happen because he refused to eat red meat. I wish I could say he turned out to be a great guy, but he never said enough to know. I've learned that mothers are wise to never assume anything. And don't expect to understand all of the choices your daughter makes.

Sometimes I think my daughter just wanted to shock me into seeing her differently. Maybe she needed to prove to me she had a mind of her own and a life separate from mine. And, then again, maybe she just needed to prove it to herself.

Steer Her in the Right Direction

Most mothers hope their daughters will choose their friends wisely and run in "safe" circles of peers. They want to protect their daughters from experiencing hurt and disappointment in the relationships they enter into. You may feel helpless at times to know how to steer your daughter in all the right directions.

What to Do and What Not to Do

★ Don't panic if your daughter chooses a group or friend you don't approve of. Instead stimulate your daughter's own thoughts about her judgment before you share yours.

★ Seek reasons for her choices. Ask questions like: "What do you like or enjoy about him/her? What first attracted you to him/her?" "How is he/she like you and different from you? What do you have most in common?" "Does he/she have lasting friendships?" "Where do you think he/she is headed in life? What are his/her values and dreams?"

★ Try not to alienate your daughter. Critical, judgmental comments about her friends may build defensiveness and secretiveness. Demeaning statements or remarks often produce rage or passive withdrawal.

★ Provide a warm and accepting attitude toward your daughter's friends.

★ Be honest if you have concerns about someone. Be specific about exactly what you see or know to be true about particular behaviors you've observed.

★ Encourage her to think about all the positive and negative consequences of being involved in this relationship and the impact it might have on her life.

★ Ask how she will know when a relationship needs to be ended.

★ Set limits and enforce them if a friend of your daughter's is clearly inappropriate or unsafe for your daughter to be around.

Straight Talk from Moms

★ *If you know someone is bad news for your daughter, the best way to put an end to a relationship is to invite the guy over . . . all the time. Be warm and welcoming! Get to know him, and better yet, make sure he gets to know you really well. That usually scares away the ones who are trouble.*

★ *I tell my daughter that I know I'm not always right but I'm not always wrong either. I can usually spot the guys that are going to either break her heart or be a terrible influence on her. If someone's rude, phony, or there's another problem going on, you can usually spot it if you spend enough time with him or her.*

★ *I invite anyone my daughter wants to go out with over for dinner first. If I think there's an alcohol, drug, or anger problem, I tell my daughter up front exactly why I think that. Also, if there's a significant age difference or he's too possessive of her, I point that out. I encourage her to reconsider her decision to go out with him, and then rethink my decision of whether or not to let her date him.*

★ *I want my daughter to know how to raise her antenna around people she comes into contact with. How can she learn to read red flags about behaviors if someone doesn't show her what they look like? So that's what I try and do. It's important self-protection.*

★ *I try not to sound mean or critical of people I don't approve of. Instead I explain in a matter-of-fact way what I think might be up with them. I also let my daughter know that I understand she knows this person better than I do. I tell her that her insight and feelings are just as important to listen to as what I have to say. I want her to learn to trust and rely on her feelings. First impressions and gut feelings are important to know how to listen to.*

★ *The main thing is you have to care about your daughter's friends. Get to know them and stay informed. If your home is a welcoming place for teens, you have a better chance of building relationships with all of them. It makes a difference.*

THROUGH THICK AND THIN

Good friends can be an anchor through times of stress and change. Unlike the friendships your daughter shared in younger years, her friendships during adolescence can grow more durable and stable. Because of this growing commitment and loyalty, teens are in the unique position of helping each other adapt to all the trials and tribulations encountered while crossing over the bridge.

Teenage girls need each other, especially in times of turmoil. Some of the best support and guidance can come from your daughter's closest friends. It's often the words of a friend, not an adult, that turn adolescent girls away from dangerous behaviors. A fifteen-year-old girl said this:

My best friend tried to warn me, but I kept making stupid choices. I even started ignoring her because I wanted to hang out with a new group she didn't like. I started doing things I didn't believe in, until I ended up at a party and a guy almost raped me. I told my best friend what happened and she steered me back on the right path. I'll never be disloyal to our friendship again. She's there for me, through thick and thin.

Many female friendships tend to be close. Friends at this age become confidants. Teenage girls look for loyalty and trust from one another. They want to be able to share their deepest thoughts and feelings without ridicule or betrayal. But adolescents also look for friends who share a common outlook and sense of humor and values. It's not uncommon for teenage girls to find "soul mates" with whom they deeply connect in all parts of their lives. Some of these friendships will continue throughout a woman's life, as was true in my own case. I met my friend Maureen when I was barely thirteen.

The first day we connected, I knew I had found a best friend. We were in school together for just one year, and then she moved away. But we never lost our connection. There was such a permanent bond between us that we knew it was there for life. We're both in our mid-forties now, and every time we talk or visit each other, it's as if we've never been separated. We pick up right where we always left off. The sense of humor and spiritual connection we discovered is as fresh and constant today as it was back in the sixth grade.

It's important not to underestimate the power of your daughter's friendships. They can serve her in many valuable ways. Through the friendships she develops in her teen years, she can learn healthy ways to establish adult intimacy.

Acceptance: Belonging to a Group

Not only do girls search for individual friends they can trust; they generally seek out groups of peers who will accept them as well. Peers in groups may lead each other into trouble in periods of uncertainty, but they can also be a source of strength and encouragement to one another. Peer pressure can be positive when the social pressure to conform to certain behaviors, dress, and attitudes encourages a teen's sense of belonging. Being part of a group seems to ease distress, may promote higher grades, and can encourage positive activities.

Being a part of a group can help your daughter find stability and offer her the opportunity to practice interpersonal skills with equals. There are areas of your daughter's life that you can focus on to help improve or develop her readiness for group interactions.

What You Can Do

★ *Help your daughter strengthen her conversational ability.* Let your daughter talk on the phone. It may be a source of aggravation to you sometimes, but long phone conversations with friends let her practice expressing herself. It's beneficial for teens to have time to experience in-depth conversations with peers.

You can also help develop your daughter's communication skills at the dinner table by introducing fun topics to discuss. Perhaps keep a jar handy that's filled with interesting questions. Design them so they make everyone think and express interesting parts of themselves when they answer. Go around the table and take turns responding.

★ *Encourage empathy.* Help your daughter practice putting herself in someone else's shoes. Talk about how certain life events may have affected someone, and how this person might feel. Focusing on stories in the news may be an easy way to begin practicing this.

★ *Help your daughter become more poised.* Feeling confident is easier for teens when they are composed and carry self-assurance in their step. This doesn't mean you have to stack books on your daughter's head and watch her perform a balancing act, but helping her grow confident might mean helping her feel better about her appearance and physical ability. Some girls benefit from taking classes that focus on dance, sports, or modeling. Many find they are able to conquer most of their feelings of self-consciousness doing self-improvement activities they enjoy.

REJECTION: NOT FEELING GOOD ENOUGH

Making friends does not come easily or naturally to all girls. Some teens may feel more awkward and tense in social situations and find it difficult to communicate easily with others. Lack of self-esteem also contributes to feelings of isolation and pangs of loneliness.

At times, teenage girls can be extremely cruel to one another. Cliques of friends may evaluate, judge, and criticize others outside their circle. Girls who may try to join in may be subjected to rude comments and icy stares. Whether you're "in" or "out" can change on a daily basis, but some girls find themselves painfully "out" throughout much of their adolescence. A teenage girl describes the angst of feeling let down by relationships in the following poem, entitled "Un named."

> *What hurts you so much*
> *That your eyes reflect the pain*
> *What is it that holds you captive*
> *And keeps you under chains*
> *How many people in your life*
> *Do you feel abandoned you*
> *How many times have you asked why*
> *They hurt you like they do*
> *Is it hard for you now*
> *To reach out with your heart*

Is it because you find no reason to
Or you don't
Know where to start
Do you feel like there is no one
For you to hold on to
Do you think that if you let them in
They won't be there for you
Have you tried so hard to put
The past where it belongs
Have you asked yourself a million times
What was it that I did wrong?

Mothers can never take the place of teenage friends. However, the relationship you share with your daughter can help in times of rejection. You have the opportunity to be a witness to her pain and a resource for solutions.

Straight Talk from Moms

★   *My daughter has always had trouble fitting into groups. I try to help her understand why it's happening to her if I can. I told her I know how much it hurts to be ignored. There are friends who say "hello" to her in outside social situations but not in the school halls.*

★   *There are so many different cliques and the girls are not as friendly to each other in middle school. They're actually competing for friends! I tell my daughter the only thing she has to do is make a choice about how she is going to handle herself. And to go on being friendly to everyone. It pays off eventually. But these years are tough to get through.*

★   *When my daughter comes home in a bad mood and is tearful, I can be pretty certain that something has hurt her tremendously and that she's probably had a rough day at school. She is extremely sensitive to what other kids say about her at school. She values what friends think of her so much. But I never blame anybody for the way she's feeling. I want her to hear from me that "blaming" others is not the answer to problems.*

★   *Everyone's social skills are so awful at this age. It's so difficult. Everyone's trying so hard to be like everyone else and nobody knows that the other person is trying to be exactly like them! They just need to mature. They don't have the intellectual and emotional maturity to understand that that's what's going on. In the meantime, I try to help my daughter understand how normal all this is and I ask her what I can do to support her confidence in herself. Sometimes it's just a matter of listening.*

★ *When girls aren't confident in who they are, they try to be a little of everybody. I think that's okay. Girls need to test the waters and try on different ways of being before they finally decide to accept who they are. I encourage my daughter to express herself in different ways and to keep trying new things until she finds herself.*

★ *I remind my daughter that nobody feels like they're just right.*

Fitting In

A mother shares how she helped her thirteen-year-old daughter when she felt left out and lonely at school:

The first thing I did was to show her that I really understood what she was feeling. I told her, "I understand how difficult this is. It's so uncomfortable to feel all alone when everyone else is in groups and having fun together." I reminded her of what a great person and friend she is. I told her, "What you need to remember is that you are a good friend. You're pretty, smart, and fun-loving, too." And then I began to ask some questions to see if there was something she could do differently. I asked her, "What are you doing in your free time in the classroom, when you feel the most alone?" She told me she would hurry, pull out a book, and start reading! I explained how that might look unfriendly to others. I told her, "You don't mean to be unfriendly—you're meaning to protect yourself—but other people interpret that as you don't need or want them and that you don't want to be friendly." Then we came up with some ideas for what she could do differently. She agreed to try to talk to somebody once instead of reading her book. She thought of a girl she thought she might be able to say something to. The first day she couldn't do it. But the second day she did. Three days after that, she found her niche. She was part of a group of friends and was happy again.

The mother in the above example used four basic steps to help her daughter find a way to feel more comfortable and to find a way to "fit in." You can guide your daughter in the same way using these steps to help her think through a problem and find a solution.

What You Can Do

Empathize. This is the essential first step in helping girls work through difficult or crisis situations with friendships. Listen carefully, so you can understand her situation and the full range of her feelings.

Reinforce. Help build your daughter back up. When feelings are hurt, self-esteem weakens. Help her see the whole picture of her life, not just the view from one painful experience. Remind her honestly and genuinely of the strengths and qualities that make her special.

Give direction. Help your daughter solve her own problem. This part of the process might require some detective work on your part. Your daughter's situation may not always be "everybody else's fault." Ask her, "What can you do differently? What might you change about yourself to help this situation come out better next time?"

Come up with a plan. Help your daughter identify what it is she will do to solve the problem or simply cope with the situation if she's unlikely to change it. Let her lay out all the choices and options and discuss the pros and cons of each.

What You Can Say

★ "I think you should stretch yourself. You have a right to have fun even if you do feel ignored. Experiment. Try something different and see what happens."

★ "I am confident that you can handle yourself in this situation, even if you feel uncomfortable."

★ "You have a great personality and a warm heart. You're friendly and a good friend to a lot of people. You know how to be around anyone you want."

★ "When you feel like you don't fit in, behave as if you did."

★ "When you feel self-conscious, act as if you aren't."

★ "Be nice to everyone and have your own fun."

CONFIDENT AND ASSERTIVE

Most mothers say they want to help their daughters learn how to come to relationships from a position of strength and confidence. Self-confidence, or the lack of it, can affect the quality of your daughter's interpersonal relationships. A strong sense of self almost always improves the quality of an adolescent girl's interpersonal relationships. When teens are able to look out for their own needs, as well as the needs of others, they strengthen integrity and self-worth. A strong sense of self protects girls in potentially dangerous relationships and can serve as an internal guide for them the rest of their lives.

The mother of a fifteen-year-old girl said this: "My daughter doesn't defer to other people, even the athletic guys she plays soccer with. She's feisty! If they say you can't do this, you can't do that, blah, blah, blah, because you're a girl, she becomes incensed! She knows who she is and what she is capable of doing! When girls defer to guys or peers in order to be accepted, they give a part of themselves away."

Girls who aren't the "feisty" type may experience a great deal of anxiety and awkwardness in social situations. Because they feel so uneasy, they may withdraw and avoid others or put on a false front to try and fit in. Social isolation is painful, and when adolescents try to be someone they're not, they usually end up reinforcing a negative self-concept about themselves. The degree of self-consciousness and embarrassment in social situations can decrease when confidence increases and teens are willing and able to share their true thoughts and feelings openly with others.

Finding Her Voice, Speaking Her Mind

All teenagers experience periods when their self-confidence is weakened or temporarily depleted. Getting involved with the wrong crowd, moving to a new school or city, receiving a poor report card, or breaking up with a boyfriend are just a few examples of disruptive experiences. At any point in your daughter's development, however, you can help her recover and improve her self-confidence, approach people with healthy expectations and direct communication, and strengthen her assertiveness, leadership skills, and sense of integrity. Ultimately *she* must make the decision to find her voice and speak her mind, but the ways you respond to her can make a difference.

What You Can Say

★ "Don't defer to others. When you want others to like you, it's tempting to bury your own wants and needs in favor of someone else's. Sometimes when that happens you may discount your true thoughts, feelings, or abilities because you inaccurately believe someone else is right or better than you."

★ "Be yourself. Don't try to shape your behavior into what you think others will approve of if it means you are not being true to yourself. In the long run, it will be harder to continue being someone you aren't."

★ "Support your friends. The best way to build and deepen your friendships is to take the time to support your friends the way you want to be supported by them. Mutual encouragement and assistance builds confidence and security."

★ "You are important. Everyone is important and everyone matters. Don't minimize your accomplishments or your thoughts and feelings."

★ "Develop your abilities in day-to-day life responsibilities. It's important to learn and practice basic life skills. Know how to balance a checkbook, cook a complete dinner, clean house, and change a tire or the oil in your car, etc. Though they may seem simple and trivial right now, having these skills will help you grow more independent, confident, and prepared for the future."

★ "Learn to make decisions for yourself. You must be the one to ultimately live with your choices, so it's best to be the one to make decisions that affect your life. It's wise to seek the opinions and advice of others in your decision-making process, but the final choice is always yours. Just because you may make mistakes sometimes, doesn't mean you can't make sound decisions."

★ "Be a leader. Don't hide or keep silent when you know how to step in and provide direction and leadership to others. Start with small acts of leading and expand your skills with practice."

★ "Continue to expand your creative potential. Learn more about your interests in art, dance, acting, writing, or photography. Keep exploring your creative passions."

★ "Continue to expand your intellectual potential. Read, travel, and continue to challenge your thinking through your pursuits to learn more."

What You Can Do

★ Discuss with your daughter the expectations you have for the relationships in your life. For example, "I expect honesty and dependability." "I expect my friend to be there for me in the way I am there for her." Or "I expect and trust our friendship to survive even when we can't be there for each other all the time." Ask her to talk about her expectations of you, her friends, teachers, and boys she dates.

★ Talk about the ways she directly and indirectly can express her needs for emotional, physical, and sexual boundaries with others. For example, "I don't want to share gossip with you about my friend." "What my boyfriend and I discuss is no one else's business." "It's not okay for someone I hardly know to be touching me this way." "I won't take the responsibility of doing someone else's homework for them." Notice and acknowledge the times your daughter directly communicates her needs to you. What boundaries has she already established or would she like to establish in her relationships?

★ Talk about when it is difficult or when it is easy for your daughter to approach friends and make choices that reflect her true thoughts and feelings. With whom can she be herself? Remind her that true friends will love her true self.

When mothers model confidence and assertiveness, they often inspire their daughters to behave in similar ways. When you believe in your daughter, she will be more inclined to believe in herself. On some level, most girls take to heart everything their mothers say and do. You can't make your daughter confident, but you can encourage her to grow in ways that will help her develop confidence naturally.

THINKING ABOUT ROMANTIC RELATIONSHIPS

In adolescence, romantic interests can be extremely time-consuming. Teenage girls often spend inordinate amounts of time thinking about the crush they have on someone. They can spend hours discussing it with friends though rarely interacting with the person they are actually attracted to.

The following is an excerpt from an untitled poem written by a teenage girl:

Wish upon a star
May all your dreams come true
For this is as far
As I can come to you

Reach for the sky
May every wish be granted
And live the best life
That you have been handed . . .
I will admit it hurts me some
To only see your back
If only I did not succumb
To the wisdom that I lack . . .
Your friendship meant to me
More than you'll ever know
And because of what I did not say
I have to let you go

Getting to know and feel comfortable with the opposite sex is a difficult process for some girls. Most teens say they have a lot of questions about romantic relationships. Here are some of the most common ones:

★ "How do you get over being shy around boys or someone you have a crush on?"

★ "How do you get someone you like to like you back?"

★ "Should you tell someone that you like them?"

★ "How do you talk about your feelings with someone who may not even know you exist?"

Awkward and New

Exploring the world of love is new and foreign territory for all young girls. Your daughter isn't likely to automatically come to you for advice, even though most daughters say they do care about what their mothers know. It's more common for girls to brood and ponder. Don't wait to be asked, but go to your daughter with the wisdom you have to share. She can learn from you, even if she doesn't choose to bare her soul and share the details of her love life with you.

What You Might Say to Help

★ "Instead of worrying about what to say and do around peers you're attracted to, focus on developing your confidence, being friendly, and staying active in a variety of activities."

⭐ "Keep in mind that even the most 'popular' girls are new at love and romance. Everyone is inexperienced at it, not just you."

⭐ "It's normal to feel awkward and uncertain about how to act or not to act in certain situations or in response to strong emotions. It may take a lot of time and practice to develop this part of yourself. You'll know when the timing is right to act on your feelings."

⭐ "It's okay to hold off on dating. Agonizing over the ways to approach a love relationship may mean you're not yet ready. Don't push it. You can still enjoy the feelings without acting on them yet."

⭐ "Love, romance, and marriage are not usually anything like the romantic and glamorous scenes you see depicted in the movies and soap operas. It's true that falling in love is exciting and fun, and can make you feel like a whole new and special person. Everything about life can look better when people are in love. But there is more to love than the initial excitement. Sustaining love and entering into long-term relationships are serious decisions that can be complicated. Most of what you see in the media does not accurately portray this part of love."

⭐ "Jumping into relationships or even marriage is not the way to resolve personal and social problems you might have, even though in the beginning it's common to feel that all the problems you have in the world will be solved. It's easy for people to use relationships as an escape or an attempt to fix wounds and unmet needs. More often than not, relationships end in bitter disappointment when they start for the wrong reasons."

⭐ "It's normal to experience strong attractions as well as to experience painful rejection as you begin to form more mature relationships."

The Dating Game

Your daughter's desire to begin dating is healthy and positive. It leads her to social and personal growth, provides practice in how to get along with others, and allows her to grow in her understanding of many different types of people.

The process becomes more complicated, however, for girls who have identified themselves as gay or who are questioning their sexual orientation. Mothers are wise to address the issue of sexual orientation with their daughters early on and offer personal and professional support as soon as possible. Many teens become severely depressed when their sexual orientation is a source of shame or confusion to them. Help your daughter sort through her thoughts and feelings with the help of a counselor she can trust. It's easier for some girls to disclose personal information to a professional who can offer ongoing support and direction.

Sometimes parents have a difficult time knowing when to let their daughters begin formal and informal dating experiences. If your own early dating experiences were seriously limited, you may be tempted to push your daughter too quickly, so she can experience what you didn't, or overprotect her because you are afraid of the "dangers" inherent in dating experiences. Either way you are setting standards for dating behaviors that meet your needs, not your daughter's. Consider letting your daughter help you determine when she is ready to begin dating and what form dating will take.

Each girl matures at a different rate and needs to be treated as an individual, but all teens can benefit from parents setting limits as they begin the dating process. Only you can determine how much influence you will have, but it's safe to say that your influence is needed. The following general guidelines might be helpful as you consider the ways you want to approach your daughter's initiation into the world of dating:

★ Think about allowing your daughter to begin the dating process by participating in group activities with both sexes. Youth group activities, school dances, and chaperoned private parties are examples of the kind of opportunities that help young teens get to know each other better on a social level. In early adolescence, girls and their peers are not likely to be mature enough for more intense forms of formal dating.

★ Teens who have developed physically at an early age may overestimate their dating abilities. It's not uncommon for mature-looking girls to develop crushes on older boys, who may expect more emotional intensity from them than they are ready for. They may also not know how to deal with the sexual demands older boys might place on them. Forbidding her to go out with boys who are too old for her probably won't win you any popularity contests, but for her own safety, setting limits is sometimes necessary.

✱ When your daughter reaches late adolescence (usually ages sixteen to eighteen), it is normal for her to participate in more formal dating experiences on her own.

✱ To encourage dialogue about her dating experiences and to persuade her to reflect on the choices she's making, try asking the following questions: "What is it about _____ you enjoy so much? Is this a fun date or more serious relationship? Between _____ and _____, whom do you care more for at this point? Why?"

✱ The decisions most moms continue to participate in include establishing a curfew time, frequency of dating, types of events she will attend and the partners she will go out with.

✱ Encourage your daughter to stay open to dating a variety of people, rather than restrict herself to only potential long-term relationships or marriage partners. Socializing too seriously at this age can limit teens. Instead, help her see dating as a fun, exciting, and easygoing activity during this time in her life.

✱ Let your daughter test her maturity and values in the real world. The limits you have established should be flexible enough to allow her to begin the development of intimacy, sharing, commitment, and trust. Practice is usually good preparation for future long-term relationships.

✱ When your daughter turns eighteen and graduates from high school, moms generally agree that it's time to completely let go. Your influence can remain, but your control should not.

There are advantages to letting your daughter take full responsibility for her dating behaviors while she's still living with you. During this period, with your love and support well within her grasp, it will be easier for her to cope with and learn from her mistakes. You can be a lifeline if the bridge she's crossing happens to become temporarily shaky and unstable.

WARNING SIGNS

Sexual abuse, date rape, interpersonal violence, or harassment during adolescence can disrupt the pride a young girl feels about her body and the growing attractions and trust she has in peers. Victimization can occur just as easily in homosexual relationships as in heterosexual relationships.

Your daughter may or may not choose to disclose such experiences to you. Every girl and every situation is different. However, the more you understand, the more alert you'll be to the potential indicators of these crimes. Understanding the offender dynamics and the common reactions girls often have to this form of victimization will increase your chances of intervening in a helpful way.

Sexual Abuse

Sexual abuse can occur with or without physical contact. It can be any touch or act that is sexual in content or is used by the offender for sexual gratification or stimulation by force, threats, coercion, bribery, trickery, teasing, lewd comments, or intrusive questions. Intruding on girls while bathing, dressing, or sleeping can also be exploitative. Sexual abuse often occurs between people where an imbalance exists in age, size, power, development, or knowledge. Perpetrators may be family members, acquaintances, friends, or strangers.

Look and Listen for These Signs

★   confusion, shame, guilt

★   discomfort or avoidance of someone she knows (most victims are abused by someone they know)

★   anxiety, anger, fearfulness, depression, disturbed sleep, nightmares

★   physical symptoms (headaches, stomachaches)

★   eating disorders

★   involvement in abusive relationships

★   difficulty establishing warm, trusting, intimate relationships

★   self-destructive behaviors such as suicide attempts, substance abuse, or running away

Some teens are able to tell their mothers that they've been sexually abused, while others choose to share their pain with a friend, teacher, or school counselor. It's not uncommon, however, for many girls to suffer the effects of sexual abuse in silence and secrecy for days, weeks, months, and even years. Regardless of the way you might find out, your response to her is what's important.

What Action to Take

★ If she is able to talk to you about what happened, listen with empathy.

★ Assure her she is doing the right thing by disclosing the abuse.

★ Show your daughter that you love her, believe her, and will support her. Help her feel safe.

★ Never place blame on your daughter, place it on the offender(s), where it belongs.

★ Remind her that sexual abuse is a crime; it's not the same thing as having sex.

★ Discuss her choices and options for reporting the abuse and taking legal action. Contact a victims' services program, women's center, or child protective agency for consultation.

★ Set up a medical exam if the abuse involved any physical, sexual contact, or penetration vaginally, orally, or anally.

★ To help her resolve the trauma she has endured, find your daughter professional support from a counselor or therapist she trusts.

★ Provide her with written information about offender dynamics, future prevention skills, and reactions that are common among survivors of sexual abuse.

★ Give her hope. Acknowledge that such an experience changes people, but that with time she can come through this successfully and feel happy in her life again.

Date Rape

Date rape is forced, unwanted sexual intercourse while on a date. Unfortunately, no matter how well your daughter knows someone, problems can arise. Date rape can occur where two people have gone out together for a very long time. Offenders may become more insistent and try verbally and/or physically to coerce a teen into sexual activity that she objects to.

Offenders rape out of a desire for power and control, and out of anger, hostility, and contempt. Not only does a teenage girl suffer a physical violation but her trust has also been betrayed. If your daughter has been a victim of rape or becomes a victim, the signs you might expect to see may include:

★ psychological shock, confusion, numbness

★ promiscuity or withdrawal

★ fear of closeness

★ anxiety, depression, and shame

★ loss of trust and openness

★ self-doubt, humiliation, self-devaluation, and guilt

★ chronic fatigue, tension, disturbed sleep, nightmares

★ eating disorders

★ suicidal thoughts

★ physical ailments and pain

What Action to Take

★ Listen and give support. Help her express all the thoughts and feelings she has as many times as she needs to.

★ Give her the freedom and permission to cry.

★ Validate that date rape is a crime. Provide her with information about the dynamics of date rape to help her understand the ways she may have been tricked and betrayed by someone she trusted.

★ Do not correct, judge, or teach her about what she could, or "should," have done differently.

★ Prepare her for a wide range of emotional reactions that may last a long time.

★ Help her feel safe. With the help of professional consultation, discuss her choices regarding legal intervention and protection.

★ Therapy is important. Contact a rape crisis hotline, victim services, or another mental health professional whom your daughter can talk to. Group counseling can be very beneficial as well.

★ Assure her that with help she can gain control over stressful and painful memories and reactions.

★ Arrange for a medical exam.

★ Suggest that she enroll in assertiveness or self-defense classes to help restore her self-confidence.

Interpersonal Violence and Harassment

All teen girls are potential targets for violence in a relationship. Your daughter may unexpectedly find herself dating someone who has a poor self-image and an underlying hatred of women. Violent offenders abuse girls in an effort to control them. They do this through fear, humiliation, intimidation, and psychological, physical, and/or spiritual abuse. Interpersonal violence may include constant criticism, name-calling, verbal attacks, threats of harm, and yelling. If confronted, the offender blames his victim. In cases where someone is harassing your daughter, sexually or not, dangerous stalking situations may occur. The offender is usually a boyfriend, a coworker, or an acquaintance.

Look and Listen for These Signs

★ Daughter is involved with someone who is controlling, dependent, jealous, possessive, and limits her social life and contacts with others (including you).

★ Offender demonstrates inappropriate boundaries by making unwanted contact(s) and not accepting "no."

★ Offender obsessively monitors your daughter's activities.

★ Offender is subject to anger, rage, or explosive outbursts over trivial events.

★ Offender uses alcohol or other substances.

★ Daughter feels confusion and blames herself.

★ Daughter complies with his increasing demands.

★ Daughter is willing to give up her freedom, her job, friends, church, or other social activities because her partner does not approve of them.

★ Daughter suffers a decrease in self-confidence and self-esteem; fears losing male friend or boyfriend (if she has been involved with him); or fears what he might do to her.

★ Daughter is often tearful; has bruises or marks, broken or damaged belongings.

★ Offender makes abusive and critical remarks; attacks daughter verbally on the phone or in person.

What Action to Take

If you learn your daughter has been the victim of interpersonal violence or ongoing harassment, you can take a number of steps to protect her.

★ Save and document any evidence of phone calls, visits, or notes the offender has used to contact your daughter.

★ Contact a crisis line or battered women's shelter providing support services, including legal and emotional advocacy. (They can also help you come up with a safety plan.)

★ Reassure your daughter that she is not alone and that many young women have been victims of the same type of abuse. Explain that there are specialists who know what to do and how to help.

★ Support your daughter by acknowledging her self-worth and right to experience safe and loving relationships. Describe and talk about what non-abusive relationships look like, and what your daughter deserves in a relationship.

★ Help your daughter understand that the abuse is the offender's fault and he needs professional intervention if he is ever going to change.

★ Help educate your daughter about gender stereotyping, violence escalation, and the abuse-remorse cycle that offenders live in. Point out the ways her abuser's behaviors were typical of these patterns and typical of harassers.

★ Encourage her participation in both individual and group support to foster change in her attitudes and behaviors and to help prevent future victimization.

STRETCHING EXERCISES

The following exercises are designed to enhance your daughter's awareness and encourage proactive behaviors in her relationships with others.

Exercise: Awareness Lists

Encourage your daughter to identify relationships that build her up and are supportive of who she is versus relationships that deplete her sense of value and worth. Ask her to make the following two lists:

1. Name three of the most important relationships in her life and explain the positive impact they have had on her. List all the positive qualities and characteristics found in these relationships.

2. Now name the three relationships in her life that have had a negative impact on her. List all the negative qualities and characteristics found in these relationships.

You might want to make your own list (focusing on your daughter or yourself) and compare and discuss why you listed whom you did. Discuss how future choices might be shaped or influenced by these lists.

Ask your daughter to write a description of the qualities and characteristics she desires in relationships with friends, groups of peers, a romantic partner, parents, teachers, and future husband.

Exercise: My First-Aid Kit for a Broken Heart

When relationships end, your daughter may need to grieve and recover from a significant loss in her life. Encourage your daughter to create a first-aid "kit" for mending a broken heart. She should start by creating a box that can be pulled out when it's needed. Think about including the following things:

✱ a list of "Wants and Needs" to remind her of what she ultimately seeks in her relationships

✱ favorite cards, letters, or mementos that have been a source of strength and encouragement to her from loved ones (anything that makes her feel good and reminds her of how special she is to others)

✱ photos of all the people (and don't forget pets) who love her and will always be there for her

✱ a special journal and pen to use to write about her loss and express her thoughts and feelings

✱ favorite poems, prayers, sayings, songs, stories, or books that give her hope, comfort, and build up her spirits

✱ a list of people she can call or visit who will understand what she's going through

★   a memory list in which she can detail all the positive and negative times of her relationship

★   a list of ways she can take care of herself while she recovers from the loss

You can also encourage her to:

★   Place any memories you have or keepsakes in the box for safekeeping.

★   Write a good-bye, "letting go," appreciation letter to help her find closure and acceptance.

★   Finally, write about how she can grow from this loss and why she thinks the breakup happened. How will she improve future relationships from what she has learned?

Exercise: Self-Defense and Assertiveness-Training Classes

Self-defense and assertiveness training can help you daughter protect herself both emotionally and physically. Many communities offer self-defense classes and assertiveness training for mothers and daughters to take together. It can be fun to take classes as part of a group. Consider asking friends and relatives to come along.

Helping your daughter understand what perpetrators look for in potential victims is important for her safety and confidence. Being prepared will help her know when to fight back and how. She will also learn skills to be savvy about spotting potentially abusive men or rapists. Education is empowering, and women of all ages can benefit from learning survival skills.

Exercise: Keep on Nurturing

Give your daughter generous doses of love and affection on a regular basis. A close mother-daughter relationship can meet important intimacy needs and prevent your daughter from seeking closeness from destructive relationships.

CHAPTER 8

Succeeding in School

Last night I had a horrible dream. I was sent to a concentration camp for teenagers. Hundreds of us were lined up against a wall in a long, cold cement corridor. Everyone was stripped of all clothes and belongings. I was naked in front of everybody! We were herded into rooms where an adult with a whip yelled at us like we were animals. If we didn't do exactly what they said or we couldn't answer a question, we were branded and punished. I wanted to run away, but there was no escape. I was a prisoner. At one point I saw a phone in a small room on a soldier's desk. On my way to the bathroom I snuck in and called my mom as fast as I could. She asked me where I was, but before I could tell her, a man in a uniform ripped the phone away from my ear. In the seconds before he hung up the receiver I screamed out, "School!" But she never came to rescue me.

—Diary entry from a thirteen-year-old girl

It can be frightening for some teenagers to make the transition to junior and senior high schools. A number of girls feel less motivated and more vulnerable to self-doubt than they did in earlier grades, in part because of the change in climate they encounter.

Elementary schools are often more friendly, warm, and responsive than the secondary schools to which they are promoted. If your daughter is now experiencing rigid demands, intensified competition, and less individualized attention, it may cause a dip in her academic self-confidence. When this happens, some girls find it psychologically safer not to work very hard or, in some cases, try at all.

Your home can be a refuge for your daughter after an especially long, stress-filled day at school. The comfort of a secure, accepting, and nurturing home can strengthen your daughter's confidence and coping skills.

An adolescent's education doesn't end with the school day. What knowledge she gains from you will affect all of her learning experiences. A Jewish proverb wisely states, "One mother achieves more than a hundred teachers." What your daughter learns at home has a direct impact on her success in school.

MAKING THE ADJUSTMENT

While some teenagers may become anxious and find it difficult to adjust to new school settings, others seem to thrive and even blossom within their new surroundings. Mothers talked about the experiences they've had adjusting to their daughter's academic development.

Straight Talk from Moms

★ *I've heard how girls have so much trouble once they hit middle school. It happened to me, but I haven't seen that happen to my daughter. My daughter's grades haven't dropped and her self-esteem seems high. I think it's because her father is as involved in her life as I am. I think girls need a lot of fatherly influence in the middle school years.*

★ *My daughter has not done as well academically as she used to. Since her teen years, her grades have gradually taken a fall. I have a high-maintenance child and it's not easy shouldering all the responsibility for her success in school.*

★ *My daughter is very motivated academically, but she wants to be "perfect." She also holds back from speaking up in class and says she feels stupid asking questions. That piece is harder for her now than it used to be. She's definitely more self-conscious.*

★ *My daughter has always welcomed change and new beginnings, especially when she gets to change to new schools. She loves growing up!*

★ *I think self-esteem is so interconnected to academic success. Most girls today are getting so much validation from important adults in their lives. As a society I think we're becoming more conscious of paying attention to our daughters' academic successes.*

Every teens' experience is different. Though many factors may help ease girls into new social and academic expectations, the one you have the most control over is the quality of the relationship you share with your daughter.

SCHOOL MOMS

You can foster academic success by staying involved in your daughter's school life. The only problem is that your daughter probably doesn't want you to stay involved—at least, not in the ways you may have done in the past.

The mother of a fifteen-year-old girl said this:

I used to be the homeroom parent; class volunteer, lunchroom aid, field trip chaperone, and my daughter loved the fact that I was there and a part of her school experiences. She used to put on her favorite outfit on parent days when I would sit in class with her. She made sure there was room on the bench for me at lunch and an extra chair for me at her reading circle. We would share silly comments and looks together in class and try not to disrupt other students and their parents with our giggling. But now she's in high school. If she sees me on campus, she looks the other way and politely pretends she doesn't see me. She told me, "It's not you, really. It just looks bad to have your mother run up and hug and kiss you at school." "But I never run up and hug and kiss you at school!" I protested. "I know," she admitted, "but what if someone thinks you did?"

On Campus

Fortunately, if you do volunteer at your daughter's school, there are ways to minimize her potential feelings of discomfort and embarrassment:

★ Explain why being involved as a parent volunteer is important to you, and why it's a commitment you intend to honor.

★ Negotiate your involvement where you can. Let your daughter express her feelings about your level of participation. For example, she might say, "It's okay to work on the parent newsletter in the office, but not in my first period class," or "It's okay to be a hall monitor, but don't supervise my grade level."

★ Don't run up and hug and kiss her in front of friends. Instead, if you see her on campus, look the other way and politely pretend you don't see her.

★ Team up with other mothers, so you don't feel like an outcast.

★ Enjoy the acknowledgment and friendliness your daughter's friends greet you with, especially when she's watching.

★ Don't take it personally if your daughter doesn't want to hang out with you on campus. Most girls want their own life at school. It's practice for having their own life after they graduate.

★ You'll both have an easier time if you keep your sense of humor.

Off Campus

There are more ways to stay involved in the academic part of your daughter's life than being on campus with her. You can be supportive and active in her education without stifling the normal push for autonomy she is experiencing.

What You Can Do

★ Encourage your daughter to learn new skills and take educational risks. When she does, support her in any way you can.

★ Check in regularly with your daughter about school experiences and the overall progress she's making or struggles she's having.

★ Encourage your daughter to talk to her teachers and ask for regular feedback about both positive and negative areas of her work.

★ Be flexible with the time you allow her to spend with friends and outside activities. Facing school responsibilities is easier when she has time to have fun.

★ Be a responsive listener when she feels like talking.

MAKING THE GRADE

Grades and performance standards can be a source of stress for your daughter. Girls who feel pressured to do well in order to please parents can become overwhelmed, discouraged, and driven to the point of giving up. Sometimes flunking out is an expression of anger and resentment about being pushed too hard. If your daughter is excessively hostile or rejecting, it may also be an expression of a deeper, more serious issue (see Warning Signs at end of this chapter).

The Stress of Competition

Most girls compare themselves to others as a way to measure how "smart," "normal," or "below average" they are academically. They may be teased just as easily for excelling as for failing. Competitive attitudes can be especially troublesome for adolescent girls. There are ways you can help:

★ Focus on the amount of effort your daughter puts into her work, not just her achievement. You might say, "Achievement depends on your own efforts." "Innate ability is not what makes successful people." "People succeed when they put effort into their work."

★ Help your daughter believe that perseverance is the key to achievement. It will help her become less discouraged when she's faced with a challenge.

★ Help your daughter understand that your goal for her is to be excellent at a task, not better than anyone else.

★ Accept your daughter's best efforts as being "good enough." You might say, "Learning experiences come in all forms. Even 'failure' can be an important learning experience."

★ Don't criticize, nag, or pressure her to get good grades. Internal motivation increases when your daughter is given the responsibility for her own success.

SCHOOL RESPONSIBILITY: LEARNING THE HARD WAY

School can help teach young people that every action has a consequence. Teens generally meet whatever standards and expectations are put before them when these expectations are fair, clear, and firmly explained.

The mother of a sixteen-year-old girl said this:

> My daughter used to expect me to wake her up for school every morning. Hysteria and panic ensued every time I didn't wake her up early enough. Even though she managed to get to the bus on time, every morning was a battle! After weeks of arguing about this, I finally said, "Enough." I told her she was old enough to take full responsibility for whether or not she made it to school on time. So, I told her the responsibility was officially hers from then on. The first day was awful. I don't think she believed I would follow through with what I said. She overslept, couldn't find anything to wear, and didn't have time to eat breakfast. She missed the school bus and had to spend her own money for the city bus. Then she had to pay the consequences for being late to school. She was livid with me! But the next two days she adjusted. She even started putting her clothes out before going to bed. Now she gets up an hour and a half earlier because she says, "I like to take my time to relax before I go." It was the best thing I could have ever done for her and for me.

Study Habits and Homework

When adolescents are encouraged to take responsibility for themselves, their self-motivation often improves. How well your daughter learns to meet deadlines and manage time now is likely to affect future college experiences and occupational success. There are many other ways you can support your daughter's progress:

★ Minimize stress when you can. An empathetic heart and ear can go a long way in helping girls cope with demands and deadlines.

★ Serve snacks, offer neck and back rubs, and provide a calm and quiet place for her to study. (Never mind if she rejects the calm and quiet part. Most teens can blast music, watch television, and answer the phone whenever it rings without losing concentration.)

★ Know when exams are scheduled and projects are due. Be aware of what's going on in her life, so you can acknowledge her load, check in with how she's doing, and cheer her on.

★ Take an interest in the special assignments she is working on. Discuss and brainstorm ideas with her if it's helpful or she has requested your input.

★ Inspire her academic motivation by bolstering her self-esteem and belief in her personal abilities.

★ Don't forget to offer consistent encouragement and incentives along the way.

★ Last but not least, keep in mind what my daughter tells me: "Don't interrupt me while I'm doing my homework." Probably good advice if you want her to do it.

SKIPPING: THE GREAT ESCAPE

The reasons girls give for skipping varies. Shedding some light on the motives for skipping may help you address this topic with your daughter. And if you don't already understand what girls today are doing when they skip, the following information may be especially enlightening.

Straight Talk from Daughters

★ *I'm too tired early in the morning. So sometimes I just say, "Screw it. I'm not going today," and I go back to sleep.*

★ *I have this really big fear about oral reports. I get so nervous I get sick and I just can't do it, so I don't show up, and take an F instead!*

★ *I'm flunking everything anyway. Why come and have to hear nothing but more complaining and bullshit from my teachers?*

★ *I don't have any friends here.*

★ *It's too stressful coming to school every day! Sometimes I just need a break!*

★   *I know I shouldn't have skipped, but we had so much fun, I can't believe it! We went over to a friend's house and played strip poker!*

★   *We just drive around. It's total freedom!*

★   *Sometimes we go somewhere and get high. It helps me get through the second half of the day. I'm so bored otherwise!*

★   *Some people go off campus and have sex. I know a lot of people who do that.*

★   *If I have a paper due or a test to take and I'm not ready, there's no way I can go. I skip to give myself more time to study.*

★   *If the guy I like asks me to leave school to go to the mall with him, of course I'm going to go! It's worth the risk. I love being with him so much.*

★   *Even if we get busted once, it's no big deal. I just have to worry about my parents finding out.*

★   *We forge notes or phone calls and get each other out because it's so easy.*

★   *My friends and I almost have a 4.0, so it's no big deal. If we want to skip, it's not going to hurt anything. My parents would kill me, but a lot of parents don't care.*

Your daughter needs to know what your expectations are for her attendance and what consequences she will face if she breaks your trust. Skipping school may seem harmless to girls who aren't getting into trouble. And sometimes it is harmless. However, all too often teens end up jeopardizing their grades, health, and safety when they bail out of school without permission.

PUTTING HER SCHOOL AND TEACHERS TO THE TEST

Research indicates that between the ages of nine and fifteen, the self-esteem of adolescent girls plummets in part because of the way we educate our daughters (Orenstein 1994). The following list was compiled by a group of moms who identified some of the qualities they believe foster intellectual growth in girls. How does your daughter's school measure up? By completing this exercise with your daughter, you may both learn something new. Compare and discuss your responses.

Exercise: How Well Does Your Daughter's School Measure Up?

Answer true or false:

_____ Girls competencies are recognized, praised, and encouraged.

_____ Grades are not based solely on individual test performance or ranked against each other, but also incorporate cooperative learning experiences.

_____ Students are provided the benefit of exposure to people of different backgrounds, including economic, ethnic, religious, and cultural backgrounds.

_____ The environment is less competitive, which decreases a cliquish social atmosphere where some girls may be rejected by peers and suffer academically as well as socially.

_____ The school builds academic self-confidence in girls.

_____ The school achieves gender, racial, and cultural equity.

_____ Teachers act as encouragers, not discouragers.

_____ Classes keep your daughter motivated and interested in her education.

_____ Educators are involved and offer support when needed.

_____ Educators encourage supportive interaction among students.

_____ Your daughter feels like she is taken seriously.

_____ The school is kept small with accessible adults.

_____ Every student is recognized.

_____ The school atmosphere promotes positive peer relationships.

_____ School provides your daughter with an authentic experience of personal success.

WHEN TO ADVOCATE, WHEN TO STEP BACK

Whenever possible, encourage your daughter to take a proactive attitude about the problems she may face at school. Listen to the plan she has for solving her own dilemmas. There are times when it is appropriate to step back and allow your daughter the time and space to figure out her own solutions to difficulties. There are also times when it becomes necessary for parents to intervene and help their daughters find solutions to some of life's challenges at school.

When to Advocate

The mother of a sixteen-year-old-girl said this: "I know my daughter is having problems at school, and yet she won't tell me what they are. She doesn't seem motivated anymore. Her grades are dropping and she always has an excuse. She has assured me there's no reason to worry about it, but it's been going on for too long. She doesn't want me to get involved."

Sometimes problems stem from peer pressure or other issues that are embarrassing for girls to own up to. Occasionally it's important to directly contact teachers or the school counselor. It might be appropriate for the initial contact to take place over the telephone or through e-mail. However, early intervention is very important if your daughter is having serious social and/or academic problems. Don't hesitate to set up in-person meetings and follow-up appointments if recommended, or if you feel it's necessary. It may be embarrassing for your daughter at first, but if you approach these consultations in a positive, matter-of-fact way, she will accept it more easily.

What You Can Say

★ "I'm concerned and confused about the change in your school performance. Help me understand what's going on."

★ "If my concerns continue, or if I can't gain a clear and complete understanding from you, I'd like to phone your school counselor and see if she might be able to offer some suggestions."

★ "School counselors speak to and meet with parents every day. It's important to see what we can change or do to make your school experience a positive one."

★ "The sooner we can come up with a plan, the easier it will be for you in the long run. Let's deal with this now and get you back on the right track."

When to Step Back

Sometimes when parents give a situation some time to work itself out, a natural resolution will occur without their involvement. The mother of a thirteen-year-old girl shared this story:

> I could tell the moment my daughter came home one day that something had deeply upset her. She said a teacher had reprimanded her unfairly in front of her whole class. She explained that the teacher had yelled at her about being sick too much, denied receiving her homework, and that she had a poor overall grade as a result. Raising her voice further, she told my daughter if she was sick so much, maybe she needed to see a doctor.
>
> I was not happy. I practiced a speech demanding an apology and making it clear I would be the judge of when my child needed medical attention. My daughter's agony escalated when she saw me jumping on an emotional warpath. She begged me not to call or do anything. She was afraid it would only make things worse for her.
>
> I went for a long walk and anguished over what to do. How could I let this woman punish my daughter so unfairly? My speech to her grew stronger and sharper with every corner I stomped around, but something inside me said to listen to what my daughter needed, too. It was hard to restrain myself, but I decided to let her try to handle it before I stepped in. When I got home I talked to her about how she thought she would like to handle it and promised not to interfere.
>
> The next day she came home even more upset. This time her anger was directed at me. She accused me of breaking my promise not to call the teacher. I assured her I hadn't spoken to anyone at school. She told me her teacher had apologized and admitted she had made a mistake. She told my daughter she had an excellent grade in her class and had turned in all of her assignments. She also apologized for criticizing her for being sick too much and acknowledged that she had in fact very few absences.
>
> My daughter accepted her apology, but at first was certain it only happened because I had called to demand it. It meant a great deal to my daughter to see her teacher own up to her mistake, not because she was pressured by a parent but because she wanted to. I was relieved the teacher ended up setting a good example for her.

In this case, a bad situation got better without parental involvement and clearly had a more positive result than if the student's mother had influenced the outcome. Sometimes it pays to step back and give your daughter the time to muddle through a situation in her own way.

WARNING SIGNS

Academic performance and success can be severely disrupted when a teenager acts out in extreme defiance and rebellion, leading to destructive acts. Teachers, counselors, and other adults are often confronted with teens who are victims of violence and abuse, or who inflict it on others.

Though every situation is unique, the following warning signs will give you a general idea of what to watch for in your own child.

Delinquency, Violence, and Dropping Out

While acts of delinquency foreshadow more severe problems in the future, they don't always lead to lifelong problems. Too much stress in a young girl's life, however, can lead to dropping out of school and other anti-social behaviors that can affect her success.

Look and Listen for These Signs

★ withdrawal from interpersonal contact, being a social loner or victim of teasing and ridicule

★ impulsive, uncontrolled, and aggressive behavior at home or at school.

★ cruelty to animals

★ change in friends, association with anti-social groups, gang involvement

★ truancy

★ vandalism

★ stealing

★ self-inflicted violence and/or depression

★ disinterest in bonding with adults

★ sexual gestures toward other students and teachers

★ poor academic performance or failure, disruptiveness in class

★ describes herself as "bad" or "dumb" or "stupid"

★ contact with weapons

★ written threats or disturbing themes in writing

★ Internet secrecy or viewing/downloading disturbing materials

★ secrecy at home

★ substance use (early involvement with alcohol and drugs)

★ running away

What Action to Take

★ Acknowledge the problem(s) immediately and get professional help. Early intervention is critical.

★ Enroll in a parent-training program. Family cooperation in treatment is critical.

★ Engage a team of experts (school counselor, therapist, teacher, psychologist, psychiatrist) to design academic plans and specific interventions for your daughter.

★ Explore alternative schools that may be a better fit for your daughter and ask about testing to rule out learning disabilities.

★ Pursue training for your daughter in social and cognitive skills through conflict resolution, mediation, and anger management programs.

★ Encourage your daughter's participation in community organizations, such as youth service agencies, recreational centers, and religious organizations, that strengthen feelings of inclusion, and provide affirmation and acceptance.

STRETCHING EXERCISES

To acknowledge, encourage, and motivate your daughter's academic success, try the following exercises.

Exercise: Pony Express Rewards

Plan ahead to acknowledge your daughter's success in a special way when she meets educational goals or objectives for attendance, grades, effort, project completion, or positive feedback. Send her a surprise in the mail. Ideas include a congratulation card or note, movie tickets, video rental coupons, a fun book or magazine, a coupon entitling her to her "favorite dinner," party celebration, manicure or pedicure, or anything that will show her you notice and are proud of her accomplishments.

Exercise: Plan a "Play Day"

Every once in a while, consider giving your daughter a "ditch day" and let her play hooky. Plan a day off together as acknowledgment of her hard work and commitment to her academic responsibilities. Not only will you be giving her a much-needed break, but you will also be helping her learn how to take time off and balance her efforts. School is important, but it's also important to keep it in perspective. It's usually not helpful for girls to center their entire existence and reason for happiness on their academic performance. When you give your daughter permission and freedom to have fun, she may be less likely to seek it out in inappropriate ways.

CHAPTER 9

Discovering an Identity

After I graduate I want to join the peace corps and do something big. I see that for my life. I want to travel the world helping kids with disabilities the way Mother Teresa helped the poor. I believe I'm destined somehow for fame and fortune. I want to be known all over the world for my work. Deep down inside I feel like it's what I'm meant to do, like a calling or something.

—Diary entry from a sixteen-year-old girl

Your daughter may believe that her life is unique, heroic, and destined for great accomplishments. She may believe that because it's true. Great women were all adolescent girls once. They had dreams, ambitions, and passions to inspire them, just the way your daughter may feel inspired now.

For most girls, the question, "Who do I want to be in life and what do I want to do?" usually gets asked over a period of many years. Adolescents often move through stages where they admire or idolize rock groups, movie stars, athletes, scientists, or Mother Teresa. They may spend a lot of time pretending to be someone they aren't, just to see how it feels.

Teenage girls must enter into the process of defining themselves in terms of roles, attitudes, beliefs, and aspirations. It's rarely an easy process, especially living in a culture with rapid change and so many lifestyle and career choices. Nevertheless, most girls will forge ahead and attempt to establish a truly unique and personal sense of self that encompasses their own goals, values, and standards. Research has found that those who successfully achieve an identity are less self-conscious and self-focused and more secure about revealing their true selves to others (O'Connor 1995).

Some adolescent girls agonize as they reflect on the world and their place in it. Politics, music, and the meaning of life are serious issues that may demand their full attention. Their thoughts may be novel and provocative at times. They may think deeply but not always realistically. Girls are on a quest for self-understanding and purpose. Those who find it are certain to impact the world in positive ways, no matter how great or small, rich or famous, known or unknown they ever become.

FINDING HER OWN WAY

Learning to end emotional and financial dependence on parents is not an easy process for many teens, but it is a necessary step in the successful search for an identity. It's not always an easy process for mothers either.

Great Expectations

Some parents find it difficult to let go of the dreams they have for their daughter's life. Others attempt to control or direct every step their teen takes. The aspirations you might hold for your daughter could limit her ability to adopt an identity that she has chosen for herself and can live with for the rest of her life. One of the best ways you can support your daughter is to let go of your own expectations of what she should do in life or who you think she should become. You can help by supporting her need for autonomy and independence as she explores the various options for her personal and professional future.

What You Can Do

* Help move your daughter from dependency to autonomy by taking small steps that seem natural.

* Try to loosen your control or, better yet, give it up completely before she moves out on her own.

★ Tell your daughter that she has the right to control her own destiny with your support.

★ Conduct an interview with your daughter to get to know what kinds of things she does that please her and make her happy. What does she feel passionate about?

★ Give your daughter plenty of time and space to figure out who she is and what she wants. Pressure only slows the process down.

★ Imagine if she were to have her own daughter someday. How would your daughter want to help her own child find goals and a purpose in life? Try doing the same for your daughter.

Taking a Stand

As your daughter discovers her evolving identity, you can almost bet *your* shortcomings are going to be more significant than ever. Your way of thinking may not be her way anymore. She may become openly rebellious or defiant at times in the stands she takes on certain positions. She may also make it a point to reject the values you hold.

At times, your daughter may have ideas, speculations, and insights that sound troubling or even dangerous to you. She might sound sarcastic, cynical, and arrogant, leaving the impression that she's "tough" and has her mind made up about everything. But more often than not, girls are idealistic, naïve, and even troubled or confused themselves by some of the introspective thoughts and feelings they hold.

If your daughter's reasoning seems slightly or completely irrational to you, there are positive ways you can respond that will encourage her to keep an open mind, help sort through her confusion, and help her express herself honestly.

What You Can Do

★ First make sure *you* have an open mind. Can you respectfully accept and consider all of what she might say?

★ While it's extremely important not to minimize your daughter's feelings, it's also important not to take her words too personally.

★ Listen more than you talk. She benefits by airing new insights and opinions.

- ★ Take a "curious" position instead of a "correcting" one. Ask questions and explore with her when, why, and how she has come to think and feel the way she has.

- ★ Offer your alternative perspectives with specific facts. Tell her what you like about what she's saying and be honest about what you disagree with and why.

- ★ Don't get upset and challenge her out of frustration. Instead, challenge her with honest, direct, and straightforward opinions. Make it clear they are your opinions and acknowledge the fact that she may hold different ones.

- ★ Remember, most of her opinions aren't written in stone yet. Thoughts and feelings are often a result of where she's at today.

Teenagers enjoy thinking in the realm of possibilities, fantasies, questions, and dreams. This stage of identity development is a normal and exciting time of discovery for most girls. The deepest thoughts and feelings an adolescent experiences at this time can ultimately lead to meaningful and satisfying life choices in the future.

THE FOUR IDENTITY DECISIONS

There are four self-defining decisions that your daughter will make as she establishes her identity: choice of occupation, choice of a love partner, choice of faith and a spiritual life, and choice of general values to operate with in life.

Choosing Life Work

Economic status, cultural heritage, role models, and opportunities for education and training influence the process of selecting an occupation. Your daughter might ask these questions: What are my career options? What are my job skills? How competent am I academically to achieve my goals?

What You Can Do

- ★ Encourage her to gain experience as a volunteer in the field(s) she's interested in.

- ★ Support her efforts to work part-time jobs.

- ★ Expect her to contribute money to her educational and personal living expenses, so she has a better understanding of managing a budget.

★ Help her to establish realistic career goals without taking away her dreams.

★ Assist her in finding the appropriate preparation to enter a particular job or career.

Establishing a Sexual Identity

Forming warm friendships that develop over time, falling in love, social activities, and crushes are all important parts of establishing a sexual identity. Your daughter might ask these questions: What is my romantic appeal? How well do my peers accept me? Is it normal to feel confused about some of my sexual thoughts and feelings? What are my sexual ethics?

What You Can Do

★ Help your daughter find acceptance and understanding no matter what her sexual orientation is.

★ Allow your daughter to spend ample time with friends and in social activities.

★ Expand dating privileges gradually as she shows responsibility and maturity.

★ Stay open and in discussion around the value of sexual ethics.

Finding a Spiritual Path

Most adolescents spend time questioning the meaning of life, analyzing God and any number of religions. Your daughter might ask these questions: Do I believe in God? Do I have faith in a higher power of any kind? What is my religious or spiritual commitment? Why do we exist?

What You Can Do

★ Respect your daughter's questions and help her search for answers.

★ Don't be afraid to discuss religion. Share your own beliefs and how and why you came to believe what you do.

★ Expose her to resources that will provide her with more information.

★ Encourage her to attend the church, synagogue, or religious institution she is interested in.

Clarifying Values

Values are a moral compass that guide people through life. They help us determine whether or not we will obey the law, choose to be honest, avoid certain language, or use alcohol and drugs. Your daughter might ask: What is my political identification? What is my moral code of conduct? What values do I believe are most important to have in life?

What You Can Do

★ Discuss politics. Share where you stand on even the most controversial of issues.

★ Respect your daughter's ideas and special perspectives.

★ Include her in adult activities outside the home that exercise your beliefs and values.

BY WORD AND DEED

Through your own words and examples, you continually transmit your principles, attitudes, roles, and habits to your daughter. The example you set can influence her identity development in any number of profound ways.

Teenage daughters shared the most important lessons they have learned from their mothers. All of them agreed who they are becoming in the world is due in part to what they have been taught by their mothers.

Straight Talk from Daughters

★ *My mom's strongest message to me is "believe in yourself."*

★ *My mom has taught me that no matter what people say, you can do whatever you want.*

★ *My mom has taught me religious values and standards I agree with. It helps to be accountable to each other for who we are in the world.*

★ *Speak up and get involved. People can make changes through a little effort.*

★ *I owe my love of nature to my mom. She was recycling and composting before it was the thing to do. I've learned that everything in the environment is precious.*

★ *A value I hold close to my heart that I learned from my mom is to treat my neighbor as myself.*

★ *My mom has taught me to be optimistic and positive. She's really happy and can find the good in things instead of whining and complaining all the time.*

★ *My mom has no self-confidence. Like none. I've learned what not to do from her example. In her own funny way, she's helped me grow up different.*

★ *I've learned from my mom how to use love instead of spite. To operate out of love.*

★ *I've learned from my mom that it's important to love what you do.*

★ *Put yourself in the other person's shoes. Put their needs before yours when you can.*

★ *I'm glad my mom's taught me how to deal with difficult people and how to cope and get along with just about anyone.*

★ *My mom has taught me to believe what you say and to say what you believe.*

WARNING SIGNS

Some adolescents find it difficult to discover parts of their identities. Chronic identity confusion and sexual identity confusion are two areas that can be especially problematic for teens. The following warning signs will give you a general idea of what to watch for.

Chronic Identity Confusion

Girls who are unable or unwilling to adjust to the expectations and demands they feel society, parents, and peers put on them may find themselves in a state of chronic identity confusion and distress. Continued development can be thwarted when girls are unable to resolve identity issues that affect their self-acceptance and future goals in life. Note: Low socioeconomic and minority adolescents may experience more insecurity and identity confusion than others. They have two cultures to navigate, their ethnic culture and the culture of the larger society, which may complicate the task for them even more.

Look and Listen for These Signs

★ She refuses to separate or avoids separating from parents.

★ She's passive toward occupational choices.

★ She's afraid of intimacy; may avoid contact with potential romantic partners.

★ She has excessive amounts of external stress.

★ She has strong internal conflicts.

★ She is extremely rebellious.

★ She has common exposure to negative role models.

★ She suffers from depression and/or anxiety.

★ She has a tendency to observe life rather than participate in it.

What Action to Take

★ Seek professional counseling for yourself, your daughter, and her father, if possible.

★ Be honest with your daughter about the concerns you have.

★ If appropriate, acknowledge your responsibility for the ways you may have contributed to the problem. (For example, perhaps you now realize you placed too many demands and expectations on her and were too invested in who you wanted her to become.) Make a commitment to change and a pledge to support her as she steps out to find herself.

Sexual Orientation Conflict

Girls who experience confusion about their sexual orientation often feel different and alone. They are often faced with rejection from their parents, peers, and society. Finding acceptance and understanding is important to healthy continued development.

Look and Listen for These Signs

★ substance abuse

★ depression

★ suicidal thoughts or feelings

★ feelings of guilt, loneliness, isolation

★ confusion about sexual roles

★ comments about feeling different

★ complaints of teasing or ridicule

What Action to Take

★ Be honest and direct. Ask her if your concerns or hunches are correct. (Is she struggling with issues of sexual orientation?)

★ Accept your daughter unconditionally. Even if your own values are not in line with hers, assure her that you love and care about her happiness.

★ Avoid judgmental reactions and comments. It's okay to differ with her if you do, but it's important to put the relationship you share with her first.

★ If she is struggling with confusion, help her understand that it's normal to feel confused sometimes. Most adolescents go through periods of questioning their sexual identity.

★ Listen respectively to anything she chooses to share.

★ Offer to help find a professional counselor who can help her sort through the issues.

★ Find help immediately if your daughter is experiencing feelings of depression, hopelessness, worthlessness, or thoughts of self-harm.

STRETCHING EXERCISES

Complete the following exercises with your daughter to help her explore her identity and inspire her dreams. These exercises are also fun to use with groups of teens.

Exercise: Guess Who's Coming to Dinner

If each of you could invite anyone in the world (living or dead) over for dinner, whom would you choose and why? What would you like to ask or tell this person? Guess your daughter's choice and have her guess your choice. Compare each of your answers and explain your reasons for choosing the person you did.

Exercise: And Once I Dreamed

Each of you draw a "time line" of your life, beginning with your birth and ending at your current age. Think back to all the "dreams" you've had, starting as early as you can remember. What or who did you want to be when you grew up? List your dreams on the time line according to what age you had the dream. For example, "At age six, I dreamed of being a mom; at age nine, I dreamed of becoming an astronaut; at age eleven, I dreamed of being a writer; at age thirteen, I dreamed of being a rock star; at age sixteen, I dreamed of being an actress; at age nineteen, I dreamed of being a doctor. . . ." List as many as you can remember.

Look at all your dreams and think about the ways they have influenced your life thus far. Do you have a lot of different dreams, similar dreams, unchanging dreams, or no dreams? Why? What or who inspired your dreams? What would you like to see on your time line ten years from now? What will it say? Talk about your future dreams. Don't give your daughter direction, just dream with her.

Exercise: Change the World

Ask your daughter to think about her response to the following question and explain her answer in writing: "If you had one minute to say or do something that would be guaranteed to change the world, what would it be?" You should write out your own answer to the question as well. Discuss your one-minute plans and identify the values underlying your responses.

A Final Message

*But the truth is that no matter how many years that you go to
school, or how many stupid books you read, no one will ever
figure out exactly what goes on inside of a teen.* Never.

—Diary entry from a fifteen-year-old girl

It's true that most mothers will never know everything that goes on
inside their daughters. No amount of training and education can give
you a crystal ball or enable you to see your daughter's deepest
thoughts and feelings. Fortunately, you don't need to be a mind
reader or even understand your daughter's thinking in order to love
her.

Many girls say they wish their mothers understood them better.
At the same time most girls find it difficult to articulate their needs,
except to one another. Ask the question to a roomful of teenage girls
and you'll soon learn there's a lot they'd like their mothers to know.

WHAT YOUR DAUGHTER WANTS YOU TO KNOW BUT MAY NEVER TELL YOU

Four themes emerged over and over again when the girls and mothers I interviewed got together and talked about life. Here's a sum-
mary of what the girls said:

1. Your daughter wants to be with you more.

   ★ "To get to know us better, spend more unstructured time with us."

   ★ "No matter how much time you spend with us now, spend *more*."

2. Your daughter wants to be with you less.

   ★ "More privacy please."

   ★ "Let us go out alone with friends more often."

3. Your daughter really does want to hear what you have to say.

   ★ "We need to know without a doubt that you care. Tell us you love us. *Say it!*"

   ★ "Be open, honest, and to the point. Communicate with us like you would your friend."

   ★ "Take a risk and talk about the hard stuff sometimes. (Yes, we mean *sex*.)"

4. Your daughter wants you to relax and not worry so much.

   ★ "It's only PMS mom, we're not breaking our bond. Chill!"

   ★ "How could I reject you? I came from you."

Strengthening Your Bond

When you show that you like and respect your daughter, the bond you share can't help but grow stronger. The mother of two teenage girls said this: "I like my daughters as people. They'd be my friends even if they weren't my daughters because they're such neat women." It's important for your daughter to feel your genuine love for her.

What You Can Do

★ Keep learning from other moms.

★ Have good conversations with your daughter on the way to the mall.

★ Focus totally on her. Plan special time with her alone.

★ Take her camping or somewhere in the middle of nowhere so all she can do is focus on you.

★ Talk about daily advice columns in the newspaper together. Ask her perspective on current events or issues.

★ Include her in your next conversation with your adult friend.

★ Do something together to help someone in need.

★ If she loses your trust, give it back as soon as you can.

★ Stay engaged, alert, and vigilant to your daughter's best interests.

★ Negotiate as many issues as you can.

★ Add encouragement to the four basic food groups.

★ Laugh until you cry, in places you shouldn't.

★ To renew your appreciation for your daughter, imagine life without her.

★ Never stop loving.

NO GREATER HAPPINESS THAN THIS

Adolescence is a natural time of discovery. Suffering through loss, conflict, emotional ups and downs, sexual confusion, unhealthy habits, heartbreaking relationships, low self-esteem, lack of confidence, academic stress, and identity crises are all developmental steps girls must pass through as they cross the bridge to adulthood. They are developmental milestones, not "issues" that must be fixed or prevented.

Once it is over, and all is said and done, even the most rebellious teenage girl often becomes appreciative, affectionate, and devoted. Maturity helps most girls realize that a mother's actions and responses were motivated by feelings of love for them.

Loving your teenage daughter isn't always easy. Transforming girls into women rarely is. But it's a process that can be full of indescribable rewards. Louisa May Alcott said it best in her classic book *Little Women*: "Touched to the heart, Mrs. March could only stretch out her arms, as if to gather her children and grandchildren to herself, and say, with face and voice full of motherly love, gratitude, and humility, 'O, my girls, however long you may live, I can never wish you a greater happiness than this!'"

Remember, at the end of every girl's bridge will stand an adult woman whom you helped inspire for the generation to come.

STRETCHING EXERCISES

This final exercise can end everyone's day on a high note.

Exercise: Good Night Affirmations

A group of girls told me they participate in this activity every night with their mom before bedtime. The more participants you have the better.

1. Stand or sit in a circle.

2. Think of a positive affirmation to yell out about yourself.

3. One by one, take turns yelling out your affirmations. After each affirmation, go around the circle and take turns repeating it. Show your enthusiasm and mean what you say.

Here is an example:

★ The leader begins, "I am beautiful!" Each person repeats.

★ The person to the right of the leader continues, "I am strong and can do whatever I want!" Each person repeats.

★ The next girl may say, "I am special!" Each person repeats.

★ Finally, always end with everyone saying together, "I am loved! Life is good!"

Resources

CRISIS SUPPORT

American Foundation for Suicide Prevention **www.afsp.org**

Cult Awareness Hotline **1-800-556-3055**

National Child Abuse Hotline **1-800-4-A-CHILD**

National Domestic Violence Hotline **1-800-799-7233**

National Institute of Mental Health **1-800-64-PANIC**

National Runaway Switchboard **1-800-621-4000**

National Youth Crisis Hotline (for referrals only) **1-800-448-4663**

Sex Abuse Hotline (rape, incest, sexual assault) **1-800-656-4673**

PREVENTION

National Dropout Prevention Center **www.dropoutprevention.org**

Ribbon of Promise "End School Violence" Campaign **www. ribbonofpromise.org**

ADDICTION

Al-Anon/Alateen **1-800-356-9996**

The American Council for Drug Education **1-800-488-DRUG**

Cocaine Anonymous National Referral Line **1-800-347-8998**

Cocaine Anonymous World Services **www.ca.org**

Comprehensive Addiction Programs Inc. **www.helpfinders.com**

Marijuana Anonymous **www.marijuana-anonymous.org/**

Mothers Against Drunk Driving (MADD) **1-800-Get-MADD www.madd.org**

National Council on Alcoholism and Drug Dependency Hopeline **1-800-NCA-CALL**

EATING DISORDERS

Anorexia Nervosa and Related Eating Disorders Inc. **www.anred.com**

Eating Disorders: National Youth Crisis Hotline (for referrals only) **1-800-448-4663**

Eating Disorder Recovery **www.edrecovery.com**

HEALTH

American Medical Association-Adolescent Health **www.ama-assn.org/adolhlth**

American Social Health Association **www.ashastd.org**

National AIDS Hotline **1-800-342-2437**

National Campaign to Prevent Teen Pregnancy **www.teenpregnancy.org**

Sexually Transmitted Diseases **1-800-227-8922**

FAMILY EDUCATION

Center for Divorce Education **www.divorce-education.com**

Dads and Daughters (Resource for Dads who share Commitment to Daughters) **1-888-824-DADS**

A Parent's Guide to Internet Safety **www.fbi.gov.**

Parents without Partners **www.parentswithoutpartners.org**

Stepfamily Association of America **www.stepfam.org**

Stepfamily Foundation **www.stepfamily.org**

ALTERNATIVE TEEN MAGAZINES

www.cyberteens.com Written and designed by teens. Current events, creativity, education and careers.

www.girlpower.com Chat, share opinions, essays, and poetry.

www.girlprayers.com Personal prayers written for adolescent girls by Celia Straus.

www.teenvoices.com Run by Women Express. Developing self-esteem and reaching goals.

References

Apter, T. 1990. *Altered Loves: Mothers and Daughters During Adolescence.* New York: Fawcett Columbine.

Coles, R. 1990. *The Spiritual Life of Children.* Boston: Houghton Mifflin.

Diekstra, R. 1995. Depression and suicidal behaviors in adolescence: Sociocultural and time trends. The positive effects of schooling. In *Psychosocial Disturbances in Young People: Challenges for Prevention,* edited by Michael Rutter. Cambridge, Mass.: Cambridge University Press.

Fergusson, D. M., and L. J. Woodward. 1999. Maternal age and educational psychosocial outcomes in early adulthood. *Journal of Child Psychology and Psychiatry and Allied Disciplines* 40:479–489.

Garbarino, J. 1999. *Lost Boys: Why Our Sons Turn Violent and How We Can Save Them.* New York: The Free Press.

Harris, K. M., and F. F. Furstenberg. 1997. *Teen Mothers and the Revolving Welfare Door.* Women in the Political Economy Series. Philadelphia: Temple University Press.

Hyde, K. E. 1990. *Religion in Childhood and Adolescence: A Comprehensive Review of the Research.* Birmingham, Ala.: Religious Education Press.

Levine, B. 1999. Faith to grow on. *Los Angeles Times,* July 6, E1.

O'Connor, B. P. 1995. Identity development and perceived parental behavior as sources of adolescent egocentrism. *Journal of Youth and Adolescence* 24:205–227.

Orenstein, P. (in association with the American Association of University Women). 1994. *SchoolGirls: Young Women, Self-Esteem, and the Confidence Gap.* New York: Doubleday.

Paikoff, R. L., and J. Brooks-Gunn. 1991. Do parent-child relationships change during puberty? *Psychological Bulletin* 110:47–66.

Pipher, M. 1994. *Reviving Ophelia: Saving the Selves of Adolescent Girls.* New York: Ballantine Books.

Strauss, C. 1998. *Prayers on My Pillow: Inspiration for Girls on the Threshold of Change.* New York: Ballantine Books.

U.S. Department of Health and Human Services. 1999. *National Survey Results on Drug Use from the Monitoring the Future Study, 1975–1998: Vol. 1. Secondary School Students.* Washington, D.C.: U.S. Government Printing Office.

Weaver, A. J., L. T. Flannelly, K. J. Flannelly, H. G. Koenig, and D. B. Larson. 1998. An analysis of research on religious and spiritual variables in three major mental health nursing journals, 1991–1995. *Issues in Mental Health Nursing* 19(3):263–276.

Debra Whiting Alexander, Ph.D., is a mom, professor, and writer. She has provided services to children, teens, and parents as a licensed marriage and family therapist, school counselor, and trauma specialist. She is the author of *Children Changed by Trauma: A Healing Guide* and several other books for children and teens. She has also served as a consultant to the award-winning video series: *Saving Our Schools from Hate and Violence*. Debra resides in Eugene, Oregon with her husband and teenage daughter.

Some Other
New Harbinger Titles

Pregnancy Stories, Item PS $14.95

The Women's Guide to Total Self-Esteem, Item WGTS $13.95

Thinking Pregnant, Item TKPG $13.95

The Conscious Bride, Item CB $12.95

Juicy Tomatoes, Item JTOM $13.95

Facing 30, Item F30 $12.95

The Money Mystique, Item MYST $13.95

High on Stress, Item HOS $13.95

Perimenopause, 2nd edition, Item PER2 $16.95

The Infertility Survival Guide, Item ISG $16.95

After the Breakup, ATB $13.95

Claiming Your Creative Self, Item CYCS $15.95

The Self-Nourishment Companion, Item SNC $10.95

Serenity to Go, Item STG $12.95

Spiritual Housecleaning, Item SH $12.95

Goodbye Good Girl, Item GGG $12.95

Under Her Wing, Item WING $13.95

Goodbye Mother, Hello Woman, Item GOOD $14.95

Consuming Passions, Item PASS $11.95

Binge No More, Item BNM $14.95

The Mother's Survival Guide to Recovery, Item MOM $12.95

Women's Sexualities, Item WOSE $15.95

Undefended Love, Item UNLO $13.95

Call **toll free, 1-800-748-6273,** or log on to our online bookstore at **www.newharbinger.com** to order. Have your Visa or Mastercard number ready. Or send a check for the titles you want to New Harbinger Publications, Inc., 5674 Shattuck Ave., Oakland, CA 94609. Include $4.50 for the first book and 75¢ for each additional book, to cover shipping and handling. California residents please include appropriate sales tax. Allow two to five weeks for delivery.

Prices subject to change without notice.